PENSIONS

Michael Hill

D0869877

First published in Great Britain in 2007 by

The Policy Press
University of Bristol
Fourth Floor, Beacon House
Queen's Road
Bristol BS8 1QU

Tel +44 (0)117 331 4054
Fax +44 (0)117 331 4093
e-mail tpp-info@bristol.ac.uk
www.policypress.org.uk

British Library Cataloguing in Publication Data
A catalogue record for this book is available from the British Library

Library of Congress Cataloging-in-Publication Data
A catalog record for this book has been requested

ISBN 978 1 86134 851 7 paperback

Cover design by In-Text Design, Bristol
Front cover: photograph kindly supplied by www.corbis.com
Printed and bound in Great Britain by Hobbs the Printers,
Southampton

Contents

List of tables and figures   iv

Preface   vi

Acknowledgements   viii

Glossay   ix

1   Introduction: pension policy aims and pathways   1

2   UK pensions policies: a historical account   23

3   Pension scheme adequacy   41

4   Alternative pension models   71

5   Pension age and retirement age   103

6   The alleged 'demographic time bomb'   117

7   Facing the future: the funding obsession   135

8   Pension reform   153

References   175

Index   179

List of tables and figures

Tables

2.1 Relative weekly rates for National Insurance retirement pensions and minimum income guarantee for couples (amounts in £s) — 34

3.1 Estimated replacement rates in the UK, April 2005 (%, rounded to nearest whole number) — 46

3.2 Net replacement rates of public pension schemes in various countries — 47

3.3 Weekly incomes of pensioner couples in the UK, 2003-04, by quintiles — 50

3.4 Distribution of pensioner incomes: median incomes for each quintile (before housing costs) in the UK, 2003-04 (£s) — 51

3.5 Percentages of the over 65s in the European Union with incomes below 60% of the median equivalised income compared with the whole population below that level, 2001 — 53

3.6 Some indices of female employment in the European Union — 62

3.7 Average incomes of single males and females contrasted, UK data, 2003-04 — 67

4.1 Pensions systems in OECD countries according to the OECD two-tier classification system — 85

4.2 Contrasting private and public roles in pension provision — 90

5.1 Pension ages — 109

5.2 Employment rates of males aged 55-64, 2000 and 1970 — 113

5.3 Average age of exit from the workforce in the UK — 115

6.1 Percentages of UK population in various age groups, 1961 to 2001 — 118

6.2	Numbers of older people in various countries, 1960 and 2003	120
6.3	Estimated ratios of the over 65s to 20- to 64-year-olds, 2000 and 2050	122
6.4	Labour force participation rates in OECD countries, 2004	124
6.5	Some indices of female employment in the European Union	125
7.1	Predictions of future public pension expenditure as a % of GDP in the European Union, made in 2001	136
8.1	Public pension spending as a % of GDP in various OECD countries	156

Figures

4.1	The OECD's dimensions for analysis of the second tier	75
4.2	The World Bank's pension pillars	76

Preface

This is the first in a series of books on issues that are salient for politics and policy making today. The object of *Policy and Politics in the Twenty-First Century* is to give the reader a guide through a hotly debated policy issue of almost universal concern. The idea for the series came from Alison Shaw, Director of The Policy Press, after I approached her with my proposal for this book. I am grateful to her for all the support she has given to this venture and to the development of the series.

My case for yet another contribution on an already heavily debated topic was that much of the discussion of pensions policy is clouded by the advancement of special interests. This involves a market-dominated perspective on pensions, as first and foremost devices to secure savings from earnings to provide income replacements in old age. This leads to insufficient attention being paid to both the needs of older people and to the contributions they continue to make to society. An insidious, but widely accepted, interpretation of demographic change supplements that perspective by exaggerating the future burden older people will impose on society. Arguments from that viewpoint often misleadingly present the funding of pensions through the market as the only way to protect against this alleged problem.

The books in the *Policy and Politics in the Twenty-First Century* series provide the reader with a critique that moves beyond conventional approaches whilst being realistic about the political influences in play. Each book discusses the key concepts of the subject area, details the current policy models and key issues within their historical context and provides suggestions for future developments. These topical books are provocative, bringing into focus the worldwide characteristics of each policy area. They are written by distinguished leaders in the field in an accessible and approachable style.

Forthcoming titles include:

Education by Stephen J. Ball
Health by David J. Hunter
Sustainable development by Michael Cahill

Acknowledgements

I am grateful to all those who have contributed to my understanding of the issues, including in particular Rodney Bickerstaffe, Adrian Sinfield, John Veit-Wilson and Sue Ward. In addition Adrian and Sue also read an initial draft of this book, offering many useful suggestions that led me to substantially restructure the manuscript.

The production of the manuscript depended upon the work of the ever-efficient team at The Policy Press. Special thanks are therefore due to Dave Worth, Jo Morton and freelance editor, Rowena Mayhew.

Glossary

Annuity
Term used to describe a process used to convert a lump sum into an income flow. Insurance companies do this using estimates of their returns from investing a lump sum and predictions of life expectancy. This enables an income to be acquired that does not run out before death. The implication, however, is that there will be a subsidy from the short-lived to the long-lived.

Citizens pension
Pension paid as of right to all fulfilling citizenship or residence qualifications, without the application of a means-test or any requirement of previous contributions.

Defined benefit pension
Pension for which pension entitlement is calculated using a formula that takes into account the number of years an individual has been a member of the scheme and their salary (at the point of retirement or over some defined period before retirement). In this sense individuals have a guarantee, subject to the formula, regardless of the actual contributions they have made to the pension scheme.

Defined contribution pension
Pension where what an individual secures explicitly depends upon contributions. In the strictest sense this implies a calculation of pension entitlement based upon accumulated contributions, plus additions accruing from their investment. The resultant lump sum is likely then to be wholly or partly used to purchase an annuity. However, this simple defined contribution approach may be modified inasmuch as a pension provider offers guarantees of growth or inflation-proofing that

go beyond this simple dependence on the market. There may also be modifications because contributions go into a managed pool of investments for a group of people, which spreads the risk for any individual.

Final salary pension
Defined benefit pensions calculated using a formula taking directly into account the salary attained on retirement.

Funding
The establishment of an invested fund to provide to pensions (compare 'pay-as-you-go' pensions – see below). Some call this 'pre-funding'. Arrangements where governments maintain book records of contributions, report to the public on the state of the 'fund' and even perhaps invest or attribute notional growth increases to surpluses are not, on the view taken in this book, strictly funded since no attempt has been made to establish long-term investments.

Gross Domestic Product (GDP)
The value of goods and services produced by residents of a country (usually within a year). The methodology for calculating this is complex and depends upon the identification of monetary transactions.

Labour market participation
Participation within the paid labour force (statistical definitions of labour market participants usually include unemployed people who are seeking to enter the labour force). This rather awkward expression is preferable to talking of 'the working population' since that implies that only paid work is really work.

Means–test
A requirement that applicants for a pension, benefit or service have to provide evidence of low income or capital in order to

secure it. Means-tests may operate with a wide range of rules, and many modern means-tests applied to pensioners (such as the UK's pension credit) operate fairly generously, using sliding scales and disregarding some amounts of income. Accordingly, official descriptions of these tests often do not describe them as means-tests, but the view is taken in this book that the simple definition set out above still applies.

Organisation for Economic Co-operation and Development (OECD)

An international organisation representing nations committed to democracy and the market economy (broadly the world's wealthy nations).

Pay-as-you-go (PAYG) pension

Pensions provided out of current year contribution and tax income. Compare 'funding' (see above), but note that (as mentioned there) in some circumstances surpluses may be carried forward and even perhaps invested. It may be necessary to look very carefully at actual accounting practices when drawing the distinction between PAYG and funding.

Pension credit

The means-tested pension available in the UK, formerly known as the 'minimum income guarantee'. There is no general use of this concept outside the UK context.

Pillars

Concept used by the World Bank to draw a distinction between different aspects of pension arrangements. Most countries are seen as having three: a basic pillar providing basic near-universal support, a second pillar involving compulsory contributions and a third, voluntary, pillar.

Poverty
A level of living below that regarded as acceptable (unacceptable inequality). Clearly this is a contestable matter. In practice, comparative studies tend to use a simple yardstick that defines poverty as income substantially below any national (as opposed to international) average (such as below 50% or 60% of the median income).

Provident fund
A state-controlled compulsory savings scheme for pensions (and other needs) developed in Singapore but now adopted in other East Asian countries.

Social assistance
A systems of cash benefits regulated by means-tests.

Social insurance
Systems for the provision by the state of pensions and other cash benefits where entitlements depend upon past contributions. Regular contributions are required from employees and/or employers. While states took commercial insurance as their model, they have generally collectivised risks much more effectively than any private insurance organisation, and have been able to redistribute resources among at-risk groups.

State Earnings Related Pension Scheme (SERPS)
A UK state-run contributory scheme to provide pensions additional to the basic pension, from which those in good private schemes could opt out. Established under 1975 legislation and replaced in 2002 by the State Second Pension.

State Second Pension

A UK state-run contributory scheme to provide pensions additional to the basic pension, from which those in good private schemes may opt out. Set up in 2002 to replace SERPS.

Tiers

The concept used by OECD in much the same way as the World Bank uses 'pillars' (see above). This terminology is generally preferred since the World Bank uses its classification in arguments in favour of greater privatisation.

1

Introduction: pension policy aims and pathways

Introduction

This book will aim to provide a basic guide to the issues about pension policy and a critique of some of the dominant ideas and assumptions. The student and the lay reader of newspaper accounts of pension politics are bombarded by a combination of difficult jargon and simplistic assumptions about the way pensions work. This book aims to deepen understanding of the key issues. It will do so both by explaining these and by setting the pensions debate in its wider context. While it is accepted that most of the book's readers will be from the UK, it is designed to take more than a parochial view of the issues not only in the hope that it will have readers from elsewhere but also because it is important that the special features of the UK pensions debate are explored with an understanding both of the way in which the basic issues are shared with other nations and of the peculiar features of the UK situation. The case for a wide international perspective can be made both in its own terms and in terms of the extent to which comparative analysis deepens understanding of the issues in any one country. It should be added that this book has been prepared at a time when an intense debate has been going on in the UK, with new recommendations to the government and new policies emerging. Naturally these are mentioned and discussed but the book will also take a wider view of the continuing issues about pension policy.

This will not be a book that argues for some simple resolution of issues about pension policy, sweeping aside existing complexity and replacing it by a rational and comprehensive model. Of course the UK has, along with quite a lot of other countries, a pension system that is confusing and full of contradictions. In order to explain how this has come about it is necessary to understand the peculiar politics of pensions. That implies that eliminating the weaknesses of the pensions system is a difficult venture, in which political considerations as much as organisational dilemmas will impose complications.

There are thus two generalisations about policy processes that need to be kept in mind when pension policy is considered. One of these is that actual policies are very often products of compromises between people with different, and often conflicting, values and goals. The other is that policy processes follow 'pathways' in which early decisions structure later ones. These two propositions are particularly relevant for pension policy, helping to explain why existing policies are often complex and hard to reform.

It is furthermore difficult to handle issues about pension policy within democratic politics because of the extent to which political time frames are essentially short while pension policy making needs to give attention to needs and expectations 30 or more years ahead. Three short-run political concerns tend to drive out long-run ones:

- the needs and demands of people who are already at or close to pension age;
- the 'input' side of pensions (what kinds of contributions or savings are seen to be needed) where obviously current costs are likely to preoccupy voters;
- the business interests of those who sell private pensions and manage pension investments.

The next section amplifies this introduction by means of a generalised and simplified lightning tour of pension history.

Pensions and pension politics: a historical account

It will be argued in Chapter Five that, in the examination of pension policy today, issues about securing an entitlement to pensions and issues about retirement need to be distinguished. It is nevertheless the case that it is the development of the notion of retirement from employment that is of primary importance for understanding the emergence of pension systems. That is then closely related to a second issue, the expectation of a period of life after retirement, which has been vastly extended by human longevity in many societies today. These are probably the key phenomena to which attention needs to be given in exploring the history of pension policies. To these phenomena can be added a third consideration, the development of institutional devices for ensuring income streams for individuals after the termination of employment. Governments have of course been involved as key players in relation to all three of these phenomena, and particularly the last one, but it is important to understand the significance of the three developments regardless of the specific state response to them.

When moving on, then, to the responses of governments at the various stages of pension development it is important to bear in mind that politicians operate in situations in which many problems require their attention but the extent to which they experience pressures towards action in respect of these vary. Kingdon (1995) has written of the policy process as depending upon the coming together of 'three streams': problems, policies and politics. Since many of the problems to be resolved by the adoption of pension policy lie in the future, the extent to which issues get onto current political agendas will be strongly influenced by the success of policy change advocates (what Kingdon calls 'policy entrepreneurs') in getting these into contemporary political thinking.

Retirement and pensions until the mid-19th century

In societies in which much employment is in peasant-based agriculture and small family-based businesses, individuals expect to be employed until the end of their lives. When physical frailty makes this difficult there is likely to be a shift of primary responsibility to their offspring with the older people continuing to make contributions insofar as they are able to do so. Not surprisingly, in such situations there are expectations that the economic enterprise and the home will be a family concern, with support flowing from those most able to those least able to contribute.

In this context, in the event of a lack of heirs, transfers to others are likely to involve deals in which there are agreements for support or the transfer of resources. In the case of successful businesses such transfers may be monetised through the sale of assets and goodwill. Additionally, other ways of securing support have been devised. Thane (2000) reviews a historical literature that offers evidence of 'retirement contracts' that were 'agreements whereby the tenant or owner of property transferred control to another on condition that he or she received care and/or an effective 'pension' for the remainder of his or her life' (Thane, 2000, p 75).

Those whose 'assets' consisted solely of their capacity to labour had nothing to trade for protection. The standard assumptions were that they would be in employment until they died. The reality was, however, first, widespread family support, second, a variety of charitable ventures (of which we are still reminded today by their physical legacy in the form of surviving almshouses) and, third, minimal and reluctantly provided public contributions subject to strict means-testing. To these were gradually added various forms of mutual aid.

Thane reports an exception to this bleak picture in respect of some public and religious offices. Indeed she goes further to say: '"Pensions" were paid under a variety of arrangements in return for faithful service to the royal family, the great aristocratic houses, or indeed to any grateful employer able to afford it' (Thane, 2000, p 85). She does not go on to quantify this, and it may be suggested that the capacity to do this on any scale must have been limited to a small number of very powerful actors whose influence can mostly be equated with the emergent state (leaving out of this discussion the difficult and irrelevant question of what exactly might be meant by a state in pre-modern terms).

Thane's reference to 'faithful' service reminds us that, as far as these powerful employers were concerned, securing loyalty would be likely to entail preventing situations in which individuals exploited their office for private gain against the interest of their employer. Any prospect of eventual insecurity might encourage this.

While loyalty within public employment was one consideration, another was the threat a disgruntled former official might provide for the regime. That this is not an unimportant point can be recognised if you bear in mind that in the pre-modern state numerically the largest group of public employees were in the armed services. Aggrieved former soldiers, or indeed current soldiers concerned about their future security, are a particularly salient threat to a regime. In the history of Medieval and Renaissance societies, wars involving the movement of mercenaries from one state or city employer to another feature widely. Hence, it is not surprising that many of the earliest pension arrangements were for public officials, and particularly military ones.

This early development of pensions for public sector employees is important for the story of pension policy as a whole since it meant that by the time wider pension provisions were on the public policy agenda many public servants were already protected in ways that might be hard to integrate with the arrangements for others. More cynically, we may also note that, therefore, the officials who were required to work on the planning of public policies were often already protected themselves, and unwilling to share their arrangements with the general public particularly if it implied worsening their own terms.

It is appropriate to interpose here a definitional issue. In the discussion of state or public pensions throughout this book these state-provided pensions will be described as 'private' inasmuch as they accrue to specific private individuals in respect of their public employment, and thus resemble the similar private pensions of other employees and not the more general benefits provided under state schemes designed for all employees/citizens.

But the considerations about the state set out here might also apply to large private employers, particularly those anxious to protect near monopolies. Of course, another factor in this early development is embodied in Thane's reference to employers 'able to afford' pensions. Their continued flow depended upon the continuing current resources of the paymaster. The emergent capitalist enterprises of the 19th century could seldom guarantee such continuity.

The emergence of a need for a public pensions agenda at the end of the 19th century

Obviously, when exactly issues about public pensions got onto the political agenda varied from place to place. The developments to be discussed here generally belong to the last part of the 19th century in Europe. Key factors in the policy process in the first phase in the development of pension policies were:

- an ageing population and increasing employer reluctance to keep older workers;
- private employer willingness to make provisions for some workers (mainly the more qualified and skilled), developing what were in effect deferred wage arrangements for them that reinforced their loyalty to the company;
- a readiness to see poverty in old age as not the fault of the individual;
- a recognition by politicians and other influential figures of the increasing limitations of private and voluntary initiatives;
- the emergence of democracy, and the inclusion of social welfare policies in the political programmes of parties seeking the support of voters.

As suggested above, the expectation about work, before the late 19th century, was that it continued until death. Perhaps such an expectation might be modified in practice by transfers to lighter work in later life. With growing industrial organisation the willingness of employers to tolerate that option began to decline. Political, journalistic and novelistic critiques of 19th-century capitalism draw our attention to the increasing use of highly mechanised work practices and increasing concerns about competitive efficiency. While the obsession with the relentless assembly line form of employment is often seen as belonging to the 20th century ('Fordism', named after the US car manufacturer), its roots lie in the 19th century. In this context, workers whose strength and speed of working began to decline were increasingly regarded as dispensable by productive enterprises. The volume of people discarded by the workforce and unable to find their way into other employment began to grow.

Accompanying this development was increased life expectancies. There is a need to be careful about imposing demographic data from a much later period upon an interpretation of 19th-century developments. However, male life expectancy at birth (the female one is left out here because of the extent to which high maternal mortality was crucial for the early statistics) in the UK rose from age 40 in 1851 to 51 by the end of the 19th century, and passed 75 by the end of the 20th century. However, these are averages and more crucial for pension issues are expectancies after reaching retirement. In 1901, men who reached age 60 could expect on average to reach 73.

So certainly the increasing numbers reaching a relatively old age helped to put the pension issue on the agenda. At the same time, since the length of life expectancy after reaching a defined pension age was still relatively short, it made the issue of pension provision fairly easy to address, as any pension planning had to reckon with only a relatively short period of dependency.

In the slowly prospering European world of the mid-19th century (and particularly in the puritanical UK and US worlds) there was a great search for new ways for individuals to protect themselves against future risks. At the same time, such measures were often fragile. Nineteenth-century English novels (the work of Dickens, Gaskell, Trollope, among others) are full of stories that centre upon the risks – related to investment failures, loan defaults and downturns in trade – faced both by individuals and by enterprises in the cauldron of early industrial development. Not surprisingly, therefore, there was, by late in the century, a growth of devices that sought in various ways to collectivise those risks: insurance companies, building societies and mutual aid societies. These offered new approaches to the provision of pensions, for companies, for individuals and ultimately for the state. Investment as a form of protection for the future, undertaken by individuals or by their employers, began to be more secure with the emergence of these institutions.

It is, of course, the case that devices of this kind are at their weakest at the 'bottom end of the market', where people with low resources are desperately seeking ways to protect themselves but are very open to exploitation. In the context of self-help, charitable organisations became increasingly prominent, willing to help those who tried to help themselves. But they too found the burden of need for this increasingly difficult to meet.

So there grew up a demand for a state contribution to the provision of support for older people, going beyond the hitherto minimal contribution made by the Poor Law. It is, then, important not to forget the impact of the growth of democracy on public policy making at the end of the 19th century and in the early 20th century. It made it much easier to put issues like pensions on the state agenda. Furthermore, fear of unrest about urban poverty, fuelled by agitators with agendas for radical (even revolutionary) change, encouraged a search for policies that offered ways to effect social improvements without dramatic economic impacts.

The simplest way forward was in two directions:

• The increased encouragement and regulation of the self-help systems. Governments began to legislate to try to protect individuals from various forms of fraud, extending their concerns later to wider issues about the protection of pensioners from the consequences of bankruptcies and company amalgamations. They aimed to encourage good business practices and encourage private organisations (including employers) to get into the pensions business.

- Extending and strengthening the support for those outside the self-help system, by rationalising the Poor Law and recognising older people as deserving of support without the operation of demeaning tests designed to enforce labour market attachment.

But then ideas began to emerge that went beyond these, developing the idea of a collective or state adaptation of the insurance concept.

The emergence of a wider state role

There is a need at this point to underline that the pension arrangements that emerged in the 20th century comprised both public governmental provisions and private provisions. There are a lot of complex issues about the forms the latter took: different kinds of guarantees by employers, different ways of investing collected contributions and so on. It is not proposed to outline the history of private pensions in any detail. But they cannot be ignored in an account of public policy, for two reasons. First, as noted above, governments came to accept the case for regulating private pensions. This book will not offer a detailed exploration of this. The second reason why private arrangements are concerns for public policies has much more fundamental implications here. This is that governments not surprisingly gave attention to the ways in which state pensions and private pensions could operate side by side. Viewing pension systems comparatively, then, there are distinctions to be made between public systems that aim at universal coverage, minimising any need for private supplementation, and those where (as in the UK) the state role is much more restricted, with private pensions expected to play a key role in the total system. This issue is given attention today inasmuch as there is a view, particularly articulated in a World Bank (1994) report, that governments *should not* involve themselves in the provision of pensions except in the form of minimal provisions to prevent destitution (this is explored further in Chapters Four and Seven).

In a comparative analysis of the history of pension policy, Blackburn (2002, p 34) draws an interesting distinction:

> Culturally the field of pension provision drew on two distinct traditions, the puritan notion of industry, prudence and individual responsibility, on the one hand, and the baroque idea of a well-ordered public space and beneficent, universal public power on the other.

While readers should not follow the 'puritan–baroque' imagery too closely, this is an interesting distinction, corresponding to a distinction in much comparative social policy literature between the liberal capitalism of the UK and the US and the more state-led capitalism of much of Continental Europe.

Blackburn's distinction draws attention to the two alternative approaches to state pensions that got onto the political agenda. One of these took the development of commercial insurance as its model, seeing state adaptation of that as the way forward. The state could collectivise risks much more effectively than any private insurance organisation, and could redistribute resources among the at-risk group in a way that would be unacceptable if undertaken by a private company. In the 1880s, Germany developed a system of social insurance – starting with accident insurance and sickness insurance before moving on to pensions. Contributions were required of employees and employers, and there were arrangements for representatives of both sides of industry to be involved in the administration of the scheme. Interestingly, this approach was conceived as a way of increasing the attachment of the increasingly restless German working class to the imperial and still not democratic state. As contributors to pensions it was expected that workers would be unwilling to involve themselves in revolutionary movements that would jeopardise their chances of benefiting.

The basic structure of the German scheme survived Germany's turbulent history. It may be doubted whether any scheme fundamentally dependent on the private market would have got past the massive inflation of the 1920s. France and the Scandinavian countries went down a not dissimilar road to Germany, although with the main shape of their contemporary systems settled after the Second World War. The Scandinavians were more ready to countenance redistribution, setting a generous minimum benefit level and being more ready to work out ways to bring people with low levels of labour market participation into the scheme.

The other approach involved what may be called the nationalisation of poor relief, that is the development of central rather than local government-based systems for paying cash to poor pensioners on a regular but means-tested basis. When we look at modern arrangements comparatively in Chapter Four we will see how this approach remains important. There are countries, notably Australia, where there has been little evolution beyond that basic approach, albeit using a generous means-test designed to exclude only the very well off. In the cases of the US and the UK, social insurance was not entirely absent. The US developed an insurance-based system in the 1930s, but it was set up in ways that provided incentives to additional private provision. In the next chapter we will see how, despite timid steps in the social insurance direction, a combination of private provision and means-testing has also continued to be the dominant approach to this subject in the UK.

Consolidation of the state role

There has been in many countries (and particularly in Europe) three phases in pension policy making with (in each country) the later phases being very much structured (I do not claim that they were determined) by earlier events:

- a first phase in which, in most countries, relatively rudimentary public pensions were provided for only some groups in the population, along the lines outlined above;
- a second phase of consolidation, involving either the development of comprehensive public schemes or the formation of combinations of public and private provisions;
- a third current phase in which, while development and consolidation issues are still on the agenda, a key policy preoccupation is with cutting public pension commitments.

In practice these shade into each other. Decisions taken during one phase have a crucial influence upon the policy agenda in the next one, and so on. We have here a process characterised by what policy analysts call 'path dependency'. This is a way of describing the extent to which policy innovations set up institutional arrangements – laws about entitlements, mechanisms for detailed decision making and policy implementation – that, while they will not exactly determine subsequent developments, will tend to channel and structure further change. Crucial here will be the way in which interest groups are created, most evidently those who are the direct beneficiaries of the policies but also those whose jobs are linked to the implementation of the policy. The fact that pension policies involve very long time spans – for example the collection of contributions over a period of up to 40 years with a promise of payments at the end – means that these path dependencies will be particularly strong in this policy area.

As has been noted, particularly important differences emerged between systems in terms of the extent to which they adopted the insurance model. Strong forms of that model created strong vested interests, which were in some cases reinforced by arrangements for representatives of potential beneficiaries (particularly trades unions) to participate in the administration of the scheme. Hence, in the second phase in which there were concerns about poverty among those not in schemes or equity problems because of mixtures of different schemes, these interest groups played key roles in influencing future developments. In the second phase, and we are talking here particularly about the crucial period of welfare state development after the Second World War, democratic political movements also played a very important role.

In the consolidation period the divergences that are a key concern of modern comparative studies really emerged (these are discussed further in Chapter Four) between those countries that adopted more or less universal public schemes (Denmark, Norway and Sweden, for example), those that developed a more divided version of the universalist approach (France and Germany, for example) and those that settled for provisions that were a mix of public and private (Australia and the UK, for example).

Towards the end of this period a variety of private pension initiatives meant that the model of state dominance, particularly advocated by the political Left, faced a rival agenda, with the more sophisticated of the advocates of the private model recognising the case for partnership (inasmuch as they were reluctant to take on the provision of pensions for low-income workers) and the need to secure private schemes against scandals that could discredit them.

The interesting thing about the third phase (which is, of course, broadly speaking, the phase most systems are in now) is the way in which, on the one hand, the equity problems addressed in the second phase are still on the agenda while, on the other hand, a concern has developed about future costs. Hence, politicians are faced with both demands for extensions and demands for cuts. The case for the former is in many respects more immediate: deficiencies in schemes are evident in current pensioner poverty. At the same time the case for cuts resonates very strongly with the wider political climate in which the view that the welfare state has grown too expensive finds widespread acceptance (this is put as a self-evident feature of contemporary politics, not as a view to which the author subscribes). In that climate pensions are a very big and rapidly growing element in social welfare costs.

It should be added here that one of the peculiarities of pension politics in many countries was a politically 'painless' low-cost start when the numbers of pensioners were small and life expectancies were short, yet the income from pension scheme contributions was high. Indeed, in some cases what governments experienced at the beginning of such schemes was a surplus of receipts over obligations. But then the long-run consequence was that those obligations grew remorselessly. Hence, the innovating governments of the early stage often created problems (about cost control) for their successors.

There is today often a political conflict – a set of immediate problems about pension scheme inadequacy calling for more expenditure in a context in which there is a very broad consensus that costs must be cut both immediately and in the longer run. However, since political time frames are short it may still be possible for the advocates of costly policy improvements to get those issues onto the agenda despite these costs. A lot may depend here upon the extent to which failure to address these issues may have electoral consequences. Often, neglected groups have little political influence. On the other hand, policy entrepreneurs concerned about future costs have to persuade politicians that they should worry about long-term trends. Nevertheless, a combination of recognition of emergent fiscal problems by governments only too aware of difficulties in raising revenues, increased commitment to privatisation and perhaps, above all, hard-selling by the private pension providers has succeeded in getting the case for cuts onto the agenda. However, even if on the agenda, pension-cutting proposals then have to face stiff opposition from the many people who stand to benefit from the status quo, the substantial pension programmes established in the earlier phases of the policy-making process. All this adds up to a quite confused political agenda, important for explaining the many contradictory trends and anomalies in the contemporary pension reform agenda that will be explored in Chapter Eight.

The comments here particularly apply to the group of countries who went into social insurance-based pension provision early in the 20th century and consolidated schemes soon after the Second World War. The politics of pensions is very much more complicated in countries where pension provision or consolidation has only recently got onto the agenda. In these cases the conflict between the case for pension development and recognition of the strong case against open-ended and unfunded commitments made by bodies like the World Bank (1994) seriously complicates the agenda. Economists of the neo-liberal persuasion have been very active in urging the introduction of market-based state-regulated systems. They have had some success in getting this model into some of the South American countries, in particular Chile, and compromises between the social insurance and the market investment model have emerged in some of the Eastern European countries. An alternative state-controlled model was established some time ago in Singapore, involving state-managed provident funds. These are, in effect, compulsory savings, which may be used for a variety of family needs (healthcare, housing, education) as well as pensions, with the consequent difficulties that many will find they do not provide very good protection in old age. China, having adopted a socialist model for its urban areas in which individuals belonged to the enterprises all their lives, is now seeking to reconstruct its system. While in many respects the collectivism of social insurance is a robust alternative to an individual enterprise-based collectivism, for a nation eager to compete in the global economy the added labour costs implied by social insurance contributions, together with the colossal difficulties in integrating the rural peasant-based economy into such a system, inhibits this development. It is accordingly using combinations of social insurance, means-tested support and provident funds.

The case of the UK is one where the original insurance model was weak and the private sector has assumed considerable importance. Efforts at consolidation came relatively late and therefore have been influenced by this neo-liberal agenda. The more detailed consideration of the UK's recent history will be found in Chapter Two.

Pension policy aims

The brief generalised account of pension history set out here has shown how various trends came together during the 20th century, producing varied responses from the political system. There were issues about private arrangements that might be made (by individuals and by employers) and issues about the role of public policy. Hence, one can see pension arrangements as having very different aims jostling with each other:

> Pensions may represent deferred salary (on a socialized or individual basis), the means to secure long and better service from essential employees, a necessary investment in industrial restructuring, a source of venture capital, as well as protection against destitution in old age. (Whiteside, 2006, p 126)

While the above quotation does not offer an exhaustive list of possibilities, it does usefully counterpose a series of economic motives for pension provision against a concern to prevent destitution. It draws attention, therefore, to a crucial ideological 'fault-line' running through pension policy:

- on the one hand, a view of pensions as instruments of private or public economic policy, largely describable as ways of holding back returns from labour market participation;
- and, on the other, a view of pensions as providers of an adequate income for all in old age (a perspective preferred here to describing them as 'protection against destitution', notwithstanding the fact that in much public policy they are seen as no more than that).

Issues about this 'fault-line' will be addressed throughout this book. Actual policies are compromises between the two perspectives, varying from time to time and more clearly from country to country in the ways in which they are mixed. Very different conclusions about the adequacies of current policies and about proposals for reform are found on either side of that line. These are made manifest in very different concerns about:

- ways to fund pensions;
- fairness between different contributing or benefiting groups; and
- future problems and burdens on either side of that divide.

Actual policies are compromises between these.

The perspective of this book is that economic considerations tend to be too dominant in past policies and contemporary debates, with issues about adequate incomes for all very much in second place. But the book will go further to suggest that the dominance of the economic perspective leads to disregard of issues about work–life balance. Furthermore, inasmuch as that dichotomy is used in the debate, it tends – to obviously oversimplify – to suggest that we can have 'life' after retirement so long as we do plenty of 'work' (meaning here regular participation in the paid labour force) before it.

Hence, the analysis in this book will make much use of this distinction, together with the earlier considerations about the way pension policy retains the shapes determined by the first steps nations took down their respective 'pathways'.

The next chapter provides an examination of the history of pensions in the UK, to highlight these issues and apply them to the UK case, thereby offering evidence on the reasons why UK policy is complex and hard to reform.

The shape of UK policy today is then further interpreted in Chapter Three in terms of notions of 'adequacy'. This highlights some of the key features of the public–private mix, where obviously conclusions about the extent to which that is satisfactory depend very much upon where one stands in relation to the fault-line described above. This emerges in a particularly strong form in the evidence about the situations faced by women.

The fault-line is also central to Chapter Four, where alternative pension models are explored. This discussion is followed by an examination of the comparative literature, contrasting approaches around the world and setting out a few examples of alternative national public pension schemes. This is written in a form in which contrasts between the way the UK has addressed this issue and the way other countries have done so are highlighted. In the spirit of the stress upon political realism in this book, while this account suggests that there may be some better solutions to some of the issues about pensions 'out there', there is no attempt to indicate that there is scope for any simple 'policy transfer' process between ideas adopted in other countries and the UK. On the contrary, readers will find much evidence of similar problems and similar approaches, with differences highlighted in order to question whether our way of doing things should be taken for granted as satisfactory.

Chapter Five explores an issue – the relationship between pension arrangements and retirement – which is crucial both for the concerns about adequacy and for those about rising costs. It is fallacious to think that there is in reality any simple relationship between pension entitlement and withdrawal from the workforce. Currently, the debate about pensions needs to take into account the widespread incidence of early withdrawal from the workforce. There is much advocacy of the view that 'we must all work longer', as if this were a simple matter of individual choice. In any case, as will be argued in Chapter Five, the whole debate is locked into conventional thinking that the only kind of 'work' is activity for which we are paid. So issues about the work–life balance particularly surface here.

That point forms a crucial backdrop for Chapter Six, which looks at the evidence for an argument about the future that has a big impact upon the parameters of the pension debate, that demographic change is producing societies in which there will be too many pensioners and not enough workers. On the whole, the demographic evidence is not challenged there, although migration may make a big difference in some societies, but what are challenged are the assumptions both about the availability of employment and about the alleged burden imposed by those not employed.

Those arguments are explored further in Chapter Seven, which looks at the arguments about the case for funded pension arrangements to protect societies from the impact of demographic changes. Reasons for being sceptical about that view are set out there. Furthermore, the whole argument about the case for funding raises very clearly the need to address the purposes of pensions, as set out above in terms of the fault-line.

One emphasis throughout the book, particularly important for the final chapter, Chapter Eight, is that the politics of pension reform must be seen as involving both arguments about a need for governments to do more and about a need for them to do less. These are also, of course, very much reflections of the ideological fault-line. Advocates of 'less' emphasise present and future costs. Advocates of 'more' stress pension scheme inadequacies. Chapter Eight starts with a general discussion of pension reform worldwide and then goes on to examine the specifics of pension reform in the UK, with the 2006 White Paper (DWP, 2006) and the legislation that is following it.

In relation to that chapter, and indeed in making a case for a book like this at the present time, the author has had to bear in mind that there is now available an extraordinarily sophisticated examination of UK pension policy in a preliminary (2004) and final report (2005) from a Pensions Commission established by the government. The first document ran to 300 pages, the second to nearly 500, and both were supplemented by extensive appendices. Detailed policy proposals were set out – with arguments for them aiming to try to satisfy politicians, the Treasury, employers, unions and the pensions industry – to offer a practical programme of reform to improve the UK system in a logical and incremental way without undue extra cost. This was followed by a substantial White Paper in May 2006 (DWP, 2006), in which the government set out proposals for legislation, exploring many of the arguments advanced by the Pensions Commission and explaining its reasons for accepting or rejecting them.

This short book cannot be claimed to offer a superior factual account of the UK situation to that which the Pensions Commission's reports offer. Furthermore, as suggested above, while the author has a view of the sort of pension system he would like to see, he recognises the political complexity of the issue and the limited room for manoeuvre for contemporary pension system reformers. This book, therefore, offers a commentary on the issues, inevitably both influenced by the Pensions Commission's work and in some respects critical of it, but in no way claims to offer a distinct alternative to the Commission's reports. While these reports can be downloaded and widely read, few people will actually have done so. Instead, the main way in which the Pensions Commission's findings have been disseminated to the public is through reports in newspapers and other mass media simplifying its message. Indeed, even before the final report was published, a variety of leaks, some of which may have been government inspired, offered a very distorted version of what it had to say. It is already clear that the sophisticated and rational analysis of the issues provided by the Commission is not being carried forward in any straightforward way into subsequent political debate.

The case for this book is that it will set out the issues about pension policy and pension reform in an accessible way, without some of the detail supporting the specific recommendations from the Pensions Commission, putting them in the context of the politics of pensions.

Among the many misleading simplifications of the issues salient in the newspaper responses to the Pensions Commission's work were reports implying immediate changes to the date when people would be able to retire, or very unjust solutions for the private as opposed to the public sector, or high additional tax burdens. Some of this fed upon a wider mythology about the pensions 'crisis' that needs to be debunked, for example:

- that it has suddenly emerged;
- that the demographic time bomb is a critical problem (more serious, for example, than global warming or the many threats to world peace);
- that the young are getting a very inferior deal to their seniors;
- that private funding solves all the problems of future pension provision.

The essence of the argument in this book is that the issues are complex, but efforts to convey the main features of those complexities need not be misleading. Furthermore, it is essential that the complexities are set in a framework that is realistic about the difficulties of forecasting the future, realistic about the economic context and realistic about politics.

2

UK pensions policies: a historical account

Early developments

In the last chapter some general themes were addressed of relevance to the pre-20th-century history of the UK system. Notably:

- pension arrangements for public employees, long pre-dating the modern public pension policy debate;
- assumptions that other employees would work until they died, which were gradually changed as industrial employers imposed increasingly heavy physical demands upon employees;
- nevertheless, continuing assumptions that those who fell out of employment would only be supported in ways designed to enforce work obligations;
- the gradual evolution of alternative solutions to the problem of worklessness in old age, largely based upon notions of self-help, and backed up by charitable ventures;
- increasing life expectancies, putting pension issues more and more on the agenda.

In the early 19th century the Poor Law in the UK, reinforced in the reforms of 1834, assumed that employment should be the primary source of support for anyone (and that therefore any relief given should normally be in 'workhouses'). Such an approach gave no attention to the notion of retirement. The later 19th century saw a shift away from this assumption for the reasons summarised above. A more sympathetic response to poverty in old age began to emerge, but perhaps more importantly self-help devices began to multiply.

However, it was easier for the latter to offer security to individuals in the short run – against temporary sickness and even against unemployment – than to deal with the long-run demands likely to be imposed by pensions. Another set of organisations that were experiencing increased pressure were the charities, and they too joined the voices in favour of a new approach to the support of retired people. The main governmental devices to cope with this issue were the locally based social assistance systems (the Poor Law Boards). These bodies began to recognise older people as a special category of applicants for help whose needs merited separate attention to those of the able-bodied workless (although even the needs of these people began to be addressed rather differently as it began to be recognised that unemployment might be an endemic institutional problem rather than a symptom of fecklessness).

Hence, the state eventually accepted that it might play a role, beyond the minimal provisions of the Poor Law. The first UK pension legislation, the Old Age Pension Act of 1908 provided a limited basic income for the older poor. Access to this benefit was restricted by a means-test (and initially by other behavioural tests, which were soon abandoned). This means-test took both the incomes and assets of applicants into account.

Approaching the problem in this way sent the UK down a road of concentrating support on the poor, and thus expecting the better off to make private provisions. While an insurance scheme was developed for sick and unemployed workers in 1911, it was not extended to include pensions until 1925. While this scheme did not use a means-test, an upper-income ceiling for contributors excluded the better off from the scheme.

The consequence of this approach was that the exclusion of the better off from non-contributory pensions and social insurance (basically 'white collar' workers in clerical and professional jobs) meant that they had strong incentives to develop private pensions. In practice the minimal levels of pensions provided under the 1925 Act also encouraged better-off manual workers to try to secure private pensions. The development of private arrangements for public sector workers advanced rapidly (note the comment in Chapter One that these are described as 'private' in the context of the discussion in this book). Unions representing better-paid manual workers pressured for private pension developments for themselves and the larger private enterprises began to develop pension schemes.

The Beveridge Report and pension reform: 1940s

The 1925 scheme was made applicable to all in employment when, in the 1940s, the government enacted most of the proposals in the Beveridge Report (1942). That report proposed a system of flat-rate social insurance contributions to be paid by all workers (with additions from their employers and from the state) and by self-employed people. Benefits were similarly to be flat rate, but supplemented by additions for the needs of dependants, with children and wives falling into the category of dependants in most cases. Retirement pensions were included in these benefits, and it is these, of course, on which we focus attention here.

Beveridge saw this system of social insurance as providing subsistence-level incomes to deal with the overwhelming majority of the income maintenance problems arising from worklessness, however caused. He did, however, recognise that there would be circumstances in which it would not be comprehensive, therefore he also suggested that there should be a system of 'social assistance' operating through means-tests to provide a safety net to cover needs which social insurance was unable to meet. He described the need for 'assistance' as coming about because of (a) certain transitional needs and (b) certain categories of people whom the social insurance system could not satisfactorily support. One particular transitional need that was seen to be important arose from the fact that Beveridge had proposed that the new system of retirement benefits should be phased in gradually over a period of 20 years, during which individuals would build up entitlements.

Beveridge's recommendations for what was called 'National Insurance' were adopted almost in their entirety. The key pieces of legislation enacting the Beveridge scheme were the National Insurance Act of 1946, the National Insurance (Industrial Injuries) Act of the same year, and the National Assistance Act of 1948. But there was one significant respect in which the pension proposals adopted departed from the Beveridge design. The government rejected Beveridge's proposal that the retirement pension should be brought in gradually over a 20-year period. It made arrangements for individuals who had not previously been contributors to the retirement scheme to qualify within 10 years or less. That costly deviation from the Beveridge design probably had consequences for the levels of benefit set for the system as a whole, placing them rather closer to the subsistence level to be guaranteed by social assistance (the National Assistance scheme) than Beveridge would have wished. The Beveridge Report's assumption that social insurance should become the main mode of provision for the prevention of 'want' in the UK depended upon the establishment of benefit levels well above those set by the assistance scheme.

The other feature of this emphasis on a basic flat-rate, close to subsistence level, National Insurance benefit was that a situation was created (quite deliberately – as is clear from Beveridge's writings) in which those with relatively good incomes had a strong incentive to enter private pension schemes or to make other arrangements to protect their incomes in old age.

Just to underline those points the government set the UK National Insurance scheme onto a pathway that built in the contradiction that:

- while, on the one hand, individuals needed to have other resources (meaning, in particular, private pensions) to secure an income comfortably above subsistence level;
- on the other, the means-testing for social assistance engendered a disincentive to making significant savings to achieve this.

One other point about this scheme is that it was set up without clear rules about how the values of benefits should be uprated, as prices and wages rose. In the 1960s the Labour government did establish a rule that National Insurance pensions should go up each year in line with the movement of wages or prices, whichever was higher. But this rule was changed in the 1970s, linking levels with prices but not wages. The uprating issue remains a contested issue on the agenda today, as will be seen. The problems relating to it contrast strongly with the situations in social insurance systems elsewhere in Europe where uprating rules were embedded from the start.

In the light of the subsequent history of the Beveridge scheme there is a need to look very carefully at the way it dealt with the family. Beveridge adopted an approach to provisions for married women, which has now been rendered out of date both by modern forms of behaviour and by modern values. The Report argues:

> the Plan for Social Security treats married women as a special insurance class of occupied persons and treats man and wife as a team. It makes the standard rate benefit or pension that for a man and a wife, subject to reduction if there is no wife or if there is a wife who is also gainfully occupied. It reserves the description of 'adult dependant' for one who is dependant on an insured person but is not the wife of that person. It treats a man's contributions as made on behalf of himself and his wife, as for a team each of whose partners is equally essential and it gives benefit as for the team. (Beveridge, 1942, p 49, para 107)

Beveridge was prepared to see a situation in which married women did not work for money as 'normal', and to argue that in the exceptional circumstances in which such women were employed, any benefit incomes they received should only be seen as a small addition to the family income. They could be allowed, therefore, to pay lower contributions, and in practice what was adopted was an option (later phased out) that made it possible for married women to choose not to pay contributions at all. Such an arrangement obviously fits ill with the situation of our own day in which most married women are economically active.

Beveridge did recognise that situations of family break-up posed problems for his scheme. In the more straightforward case of widowhood the benefit system was devised to be founded upon the contributions of deceased husbands. The Beveridge Report also discussed the possibility of an insurance benefit to meet circumstances of family breakdown other than through death, but came up with no practical recommendation. Instead, provision for separated women was made within the social assistance scheme.

From Beveridge to Blair: 1940s–1990s

The Pensions Commission (2005, p 117) makes the following comment on the implications of the pension reforms of the 1940s:

> While most of Europe and the US developed state earnings-related pension schemes in the early and mid-20th century, the 1942 Beveridge Report and post-war governments established a flat-rate state pension scheme. This reflected the significant prior existence of private pensions provided by insurance companies and of occupational schemes provided by companies and by the government itself as an employer. The decision to keep the state system flat-rate in turn stimulated the further development of these alternative forms of provision....
>
> It was clear however that this voluntary system left many gaps, particularly among employees of small and medium-sized firms. It also provided poorly for people with interrupted employment records (in particular women) or people who moved between jobs, who were disadvantaged by final salary schemes which provided limited leavers' rights.

In the 1950s a political debate emerged about the need for some kind of 'national superannuation' scheme to enable individuals to make contributions to secure a public pension larger than the Beveridge minimum. The Labour opposition had been working on a proposal for a graduated pension scheme to enable pensions to be improved with funds drawn from increased contributions by individuals. The government responded by enacting its own, very limited, version of such a scheme, enabling individuals without any private pension provisions to contribute to a graduated pension scheme, through which they would slowly accumulate rather limited enhancements to the basic scheme.

On the other hand, the development of private pensions systems was evident. By 1963 about 48% of employees were enrolled in occupational pension schemes (Lynes, 1997, p 323). The encouragement of private pension schemes was seen as an alternative way, with no cost to the government, to deal with low incomes in old age.

The Labour Party came to power in 1964 and set to work to try to develop a more universal 'national superannuation scheme', which would extend a state system of graduated pensions offering benefits comparable, in terms of their ratio to past earnings (or, so-called, replacement income levels), to private pensions. In practice, it moved very slowly on this issue, finding it very difficult to confront the awkward political problem about the relationship between a scheme that would only provide enhanced benefits in the long run and the strong demand for pension improvement in the short run. The 1964-70 Labour government was still working on legislation on this subject when it lost the general election in 1970.

After 1970 the new Conservative government moved slowly towards a limited additional pension scheme, which would gradually enhance its earlier earnings-related scheme, passing a new Social Security Act in 1973, which had not been implemented when the government fell from power in 1974. On return to government, Labour enacted the Social Security Pensions Act of 1975, which replaced the 1973 Act and provided for an earnings-related

---

superannuation scheme, known as the State Earnings Related Pension Scheme (SERPS). This measure involved allowing individuals who were already in private schemes adjudged by the government to be adequate to opt out of the state scheme, but provided an enhanced state scheme for all other working people. This was essentially a superannuation scheme in which contributions would determine benefits, with inflation proofing provided by the government. It also included provision to enable allowances to be made for working women whose periods in employment might be broken by periods of 'family responsibilities'. It is important to note that this scheme was, like the flat-rate scheme upon which it was built, a scheme managed, as far as the government was concerned, on a 'pay as you go' basis without any proposals to invest any surplus. The initial surplus enabled some improvements to be made to the basic pension scheme, since at its inception the new scheme involved the government in collecting in very much more than it was paying out. It had the effect of easing pressure on the social security budget in the short run, but provided the long-run threat of a situation in which demands upon the scheme might be seriously out of line with contributions going in.

It is important to note here that the efforts to protect people with family responsibilities better during this period need to be contextualised by the fact that Beveridge's notion of the wife as a 'dependant', who need not be an insurance contributor, had come under attack for its sexist assumptions. In the face of growing female labour market participation the married woman's option not to pay contributions began to be phased out. At the same time the provision for a dependent wife (and exceptionally under-working-age children) continued to exist within the basic state pension scheme.

While that may be seen to be an anomaly resulting from piecemeal change, another anomaly crept in when, in the 1960s, the basis of employees' contributions was changed from flat rate to graduated. This could be seen as justified by the development of various graduated benefits but then later graduated sickness and unemployment benefits were abolished. The key point is that at this period the UK was moving further and further away from a social insurance system in which there was any recognisable equivalence between what people paid in and what they got out.

After 1979 Margaret Thatcher's Conservative government began to seek ways to cut social security expenditure. As noted earlier, the rule determining annual rises for the levels of pensions so that they went up with either earnings or prices, whichever was higher, which the preceding government had enacted, was changed to take only prices into account. This was a change that seemed slight at the time but which had in the long run a massive impact upon the level of the basic pension. The relative value of the surviving flat-rate pension was significantly reduced over the 1980s and 1990s.

In a review of social security policy in the mid-1980s SERPS was deemed to impose excessive burdens on future generations. The government's initial idea was to replace it altogether with individual funded accounts with insurance companies. The latter were not keen to take on this work with large numbers of relatively low-paid workers. Furthermore, the government recognised what heavy short-term costs the government would impose upon itself inasmuch as it would lose the use of contributions to fund current benefits. In the end, instead it sharply cut the benefits guaranteed under SERPS. Part of this cut involved the weakening of the provisions designed to protect the pensions of married women forced to leave the labour market for a period in order to attend to caring tasks.

In enacting these changes to SERPS, the government also gave further encouragement to the private pensions industry through tax relief and a National Insurance contribution rebate. It also abolished the requirement that any approved private scheme should be potentially at least as good as SERPS. These measures unleashed a massive sales campaign by the private pensions industry. Salespeople exploited fears of the growth of the older population and suggested that the state could not be trusted to deliver in the long run. Not only were individuals encouraged to leave SERPS for worse schemes but, in some – subsequently publicised – cases, public employees such as teachers and nurses were lured out of their very generous government-protected occupational schemes into inferior private insurance schemes.

This particular Thatcherite 'balloon' was burst in a rather dramatic way. After it was discovered that the publisher Robert Maxwell had been sustaining his extravagant lifestyle by raiding the pension funds set aside for his employees, the government set up a committee to investigate the regulation of the private pensions industry. That committee recommended strengthening the regulatory and appeal mechanisms for the private pensions industry, but it stopped short of arguing for a system of government guarantees for private pensions. Some of its recommendations were enacted in the 1995 Pensions Act.

Hence, in practice, the efforts to shift people away from the state SERPS system largely failed. In a climate of economic difficulties the growth of private pensions was comparatively modest. Ironically, the early 1980s saw the beginning of a decline in the number of workers in occupational pension schemes, which has continued to this day. It would be wrong to attribute this to the government's pension policy, however; rather more significant is the change that started to accelerate around that time away from stable industrial and public employment. The fact is that in a changing economy there were increasing numbers of workers, particularly part-time workers (who were largely female), who were not covered by additional pension schemes at all, while others were only covered by the now seriously weakened SERPS scheme.

Attempts at pension reform: 1997–2005

Hence, when Labour came to power in 1997, three distinct classes of pensioners could be identified. First, a group, approaching perhaps around a third of all retirees and including public servants, who had well-funded private pensions to supplement the basic Beveridge pension. I am in the lucky first group. My state pension only constitutes about 20% of my pension income, the rest coming from the university teachers' scheme. Second, at the other extreme, a group

– including, particularly, many women and older pensioners – whose main provision came from the flat-rate Beveridge scheme, which (since it remained very low) they might need to supplement with means-tested benefits (including Housing Benefit). Third, in the middle, a group of people with modest sums from either SERPS or limited private schemes to supplement the flat-rate pension. Statistics in Chapter Three illustrate further this 'class' division in the pension system.

The Labour government that came to power in 1997 quickly initiated a review of the situation. It soon rejected radical reform on cost grounds. It introduced a number of measures, starting with the first two listed below, and later moving on to the others:

- maintenance of the basic flat-rate contributory pension, without changing the uprating principle;
- a 'minimum income guarantee' for low-income current pensioners, later to be called a 'guarantee credit' when the savings credit (mentioned below) was brought in;
- voluntary 'stakeholder' pension schemes designed to offer an alternative to entirely private pensions for those on middle incomes, which are low cost, flexible and secure, involving private investment under statutory surveillance and with generous tax concessions from the government;
- a State Second Pension for those unable to get into private or stakeholder schemes, essentially low earners and those in caring roles, fundamentally an improved version of the damaged SERPS scheme;
- a 'savings credit' scheme to supplement the incomes of those with relatively low private pensions (including stakeholder pensions) but who are nevertheless above the level to qualify for the full 'guarantee credit'.

These measures were presumed to offer a comprehensive deal:

- a measure to tackle current pensioner poverty;
- the encouragement of effective private provision for most of the population in future; and
- a package to support those who have difficulty in getting adequate support from private schemes.

However, they ran into problems and consequently the government initiated a further review by a special 'Pensions Commission', which reported in 2005, and whose work constitutes (as noted in Chapter One) an important backdrop to this book.

The 'pension credit' developed from the 'minimum income guarantee' is, in practice, social assistance for pensioners. It is subject to both means-testing and asset-testing, even though the approach to the latter treats these more generously than before. The government has deliberately chosen to enhance this benefit rather than the National Insurance pension. It initially maintained the previous administration's practice of only raising the National Insurance pension rate in line with the rise of prices. The result was that the gap between the social assistance rate and the National Insurance pension rate widened significantly (see Table 2.1). The very low increases in the National Insurance pension rates attracted substantial criticism. The Labour Party's relatively poor results in local elections in May 2000 were widely blamed upon discontent about 'a mere

Table 2.1: Relative weekly rates for National Insurance retirement pensions and minimum income guarantee for couples (amounts in £s)

Rate set in April	Retirement pension rate for a couple	Basic minimum income guarantee for a couple[a]	Excess minimum income guarantee over retirement pension
1997	99.80	106.80	7.00
2002	120.70	149.80	29.10
2005	131.20	167.05	35.85
2007	139.60	181.70	42.10

[a] There are higher rates for older pensioners.

£0.75 on the basic pension'. The government was doing very little for pensioners with incomes just above the levels at which social assistance entitlements arise. This was seen as an injustice to insurance contributors and a disincentive to saving.

The government bowed to political pressure and announced a National Insurance pension rate increase above the rate of price increases, of £5 for a single person and £8 for a couple, in April 2001. However, the increase in the minimum income guarantee rate was much greater − £13.70 for a single person and £18.60 for a couple. Hence, as Table 2.1 shows, the gap between the support offered by National Insurance and that offered by the means-test increased much further. In 2001 the Chancellor, Gordon Brown, announced that future National Insurance pension increases would 'always' be 2.5% or more if inflation is higher. 'Always' is in inverted commas here as even if this Chancellor will not break his word, he cannot commit his successors.

The pension credit scheme may help to deal with the fact that people with incomes only just above the minimum income guarantee are losing ground in relative terms. However, it will encounter the problem that faces such variable income enhancement schemes − that the rules to govern the way it 'tapers off' as income rises are likely to engender new inequities and disincentive effects.

There is thus a continuing sense of injustice among those with modest incomes close to the minimum income guarantee level, that they paid National Insurance contributions all their lives and made contributions to modest private schemes only to see people who paid little or nothing being guaranteed comparable incomes. Looking ahead further, then, there are questions about the extent to which this will deter people from joining voluntary supplementary pensions schemes like the new stakeholder ones. Interestingly, the private pensions industry has expressed precisely this concern, inhibiting their efforts to sell pensions.

Any evaluation of the new contributory pension schemes (the stakeholder pension and the State Second Pension) requires prediction of long-run effects. The arrival of the stakeholder scheme in April 2001 was greeted by a number of newspaper articles, many of them offering advice to people who might be deciding to start to purchase these pensions. There was widespread doubt about whether they offer a good deal to low-income workers. The problem is that investment in one of these pensions can involve forgoing a substantial amount of current income for a comparatively low return that may compare unfavourably with the levels of benefit offered by the pension credit (or, in some cases, the State Second Pension).

Estimates of what the stakeholder pensions will offer depend upon taking current returns on private pensions schemes and current annuity rates and projecting them into the future. Both of these rates have fallen in recent years and could still fall further in an era of low inflation and limited economic growth. But predictions of this kind – if used to offer advice to potential purchasers – need also to deal with the future employment prospects for people (including, in particular, women) in the more vulnerable parts of the labour market. On top of all this, trying to predict whether these quasi-private schemes will offer a better deal than anything the government may provide requires guesses about how government will behave across a period of 30-40 years. The past behaviour of UK governments offers no basis for any expectation of a stable future for pension schemes.

Stakeholder pensions have not proved as attractive as the government expected, but there has also been developing alarm at changes being made to existing private pension arrangements. A particularly attractive feature of private pension arrangements for many employees of larger enterprises, and for public employees, has been that they are what are known as 'defined benefit' schemes, in which pension entitlements are calculated using a formula that takes into account the number of years an individual has been a member of the scheme and their salary (at the point of retirement or over some defined period before retirement). An increasing number of companies have decided that they cannot guarantee these sums. They have therefore closed their final salary schemes to new entrants, or even demoted the expected benefits for existing pension scheme members. The alternative being offered is that already provided by many of the less advantageous schemes – defined contribution pensions whose ultimate value will simply depend upon the growth of the actual sums invested.

These developments followed from the state of the stock market and the declining returns from investments. The pensions industry also blames the Chancellor for a change in the arrangements to tax pension fund gains, enacted in one of his first budgets. While this must have had some effect, it does not make sense to blame a change in the climate for investors worldwide on a UK tax change. Of course, it must have made life just a little harder for UK funds.

Actuarial calculations suggest that contributions into money purchase pensions, including stakeholder pensions, will have to be proportions of current income of around 20% to provide pensions comparable to existing final salary schemes. Of course, these estimates depend upon projecting forward current returns to investments. These may change.

Meanwhile all the remarks about the bad deal the stakeholder scheme offers, relative to the minimum income guarantee, to low-income and insecure workers may also be pertinent to the State Second Pension scheme.

It is appropriate to end this discussion of UK pension policy history with a summary of the contemporary situation. The system can be seen as consisting of three tiers or pillars (the use of these concepts to analyse pension arrangements is explored further in Chapter Four):

- A first tier, called now the pension credit, which provides a minimum income for nearly all with a right to residence in the UK subject to a means-test taking into account income and assets. To prevent a severe disincentive effect at the point where other income begins to exceed the guaranteed income level there is provision for a tapering-off effect, although it is doubtful whether this is adequate to eliminate the problem. This tier is funded out of taxation.

- A second tier based upon the original National Insurance pension supplemented by graduated additions from the cumulative impact of two now discarded schemes (a graduated additions scheme introduced in 1961 and SERPS introduced in 1978) and the new State Second Pension. The basic National Insurance pension is flat rate, but based upon graduated contributions, with full payment depending upon 44 years' contributions from men and 39 from women. It is paid at a level well below that guaranteed by the pension credit. The additions are earnings related, but with some redistribution towards those with lower incomes. Individuals who contribute to private occupational pensions may contract out of the State Second Pension (as they could from its predecessors). There is no investment of contributions and the formulae used for calculating entitlements have been the subject of extensive amendments over the years since the respective parts of this tier were established.
- A third tier, which is voluntary, consisting of a wide range of occupation-related pensions schemes and other private pension arrangements (including those based upon the recent government stakeholder pension initiative) supported by tax relief. Some of these schemes are defined benefit ones, particularly those for public employees and the employees of some other large enterprises. There are long-run shifts in this part of the system, with the numbers of people in third-tier schemes as a whole falling and a particular fall in the numbers in defined benefit schemes (the latter largely the consequence of deliberate steps to close or reduce access to them).

Conclusions

In this account of the UK story the details of the pension system, as set out in the last part of the chapter, are correct at the time the book is going to press at the end of March 2007. But what has been left out of the chapter is any account of the debate that has developed since 2004 when the Pensions Commission published its first report. That debate then really opened up with its second report in 2005. In early 2006 the government published a White Paper, and legislative proposals followed in the Queen's Speech in November 2006 (just as this book was being completed). This debate will be discussed further in various places in the book, and Chapter Eight will give attention to the government's proposals.

This chapter has followed on the issues about dilemmas in pensions policy and about pension policy 'pathways' with an examination of the way the UK has travelled down its particular pathway since the 1940s. There is some basis for suggesting, and indeed the quote from the Pensions Commission on page 28 hints at it, that the UK was sent off by Beveridge and the Labour government in the 1940s down a rocky pathway, working with a public–private compromise that was not viable.

On the other hand, there is a view that in some respects the UK has been a leader in a direction favoured by some other nations (and the World Bank): with high levels of private provision and attention to ensuring a safety-net system for all. But if that is the case then surely there are grounds for arguing that the flirtation with social insurance has been a wasted effort, developing a system in which the relationship between contributions and benefits is so distant and obscure as to make insurance a meaningless concept. Furthermore, there remain many problems about the interaction between the encouragement of private provision on the one hand and a minimum income guarantee on the other.

A less sharp judgement is perhaps to see in the UK history a brave effort to reach a compromise between the conflicting concerns about the UK pension system and the conflicting ideologies outlined in Chapter One: the high levels of pensioner poverty today, the future balance between the generations, the recognition that the favourable situation of many contributors to good private pension schemes is one that should be shared more widely and the desire of the financial market to sell pensions.

3

Pension scheme adequacy

Introduction

The discussion of the history of the UK system in Chapter Two indicated ways in which there were issues about the adequacy of pension schemes both in terms of the extent of availability of various kinds of pensions and in terms of the levels of payments available. This chapter goes on from that to explore the issues about adequacy in more detail. It does this through an examination of pension system coverage and pensioners' incomes in the UK, but also raises some wider issues about alternative approaches to adequacy. This brings up again some of the conflicts between approaches to provision that see pensions as withheld wages and salaries and those that stress the need for the maintenance of adequate incomes in later life.

There are three different but interrelated ways of exploring this topic:

- in terms of overall coverage of the population;
- in terms of replacement rates, that is pension levels relative to previous income levels;
- in terms of the adequacy of pensions when measured against a yardstick for judging what is needed to prevent poverty or sustain a fair minimum standard of living.

One of the problems encountered when we read of systems in other countries is that what seem to be very sophisticated systems cannot really be assessed satisfactorily unless we have information about levels of benefits and what proportions of the population are covered.

Taking all three of these things together there is perhaps a hypothetical 'ideal' system in which there is comprehensive coverage, high replacement rates and a high minimum for all. Specific systems may then be alternatively judged as good on one or two of these but probably not all three. But then further complications may arise inasmuch as a system with good overall coverage nevertheless offers very different replacement rates for different groups of people and/ or leaves some people with very low incomes. This broadly summarises the situation in the UK. While some people may move from employment to a pension with a minimal fall in income (particularly once the combined effects of the benefits from a lump sum payment and the reduction of income taxation are taken into account) others experience sharp falls in income. So then we see that it is all very well to evaluate pensions in terms of replacement rates but in reality a low replacement rate for a high in-work income may be a very substantial pension, while conversely a high replacement rate for a very low in-work income may be a pension below the poverty line. In making comparisons, one way to deal with this issue is to look at replacement rates in relation to average incomes (a necessary qualification to enable most comparisons between nations to be made). This, however, simply hides some important questions about the way pension schemes operate in practice.

These remarks thus highlight the key issues about pension adequacy, about, of course, replacement rates and the extent of coverage but also about how these two interact. Hence, there are questions to be considered about pensioner poverty, and about inequity in terms of the very different deals pension systems offer different individuals. At the same time there are also important political questions about the returns individuals acquire from their contributions.

It is necessary to order this discussion, since we cannot consider everything at the same time, in a way that may sometimes seem to separate out these different issues. It will start with some of the issues about replacement levels. Then it will consider issues about inclusiveness. This logically needs to be explored in terms of issues of current or potential pensioner poverty and consequences of shortfalls in either the levels of pensions or their availability or perhaps both. Finally, the special issues about the treatment of women by pension schemes will be considered, involving all of the considerations already examined but with special features consequent upon either assumptions about family life or forms of female labour market participation or of course both.

Replacement levels

Pension arrangements are often compared in terms of pension rates relative to earnings, talking about amounts paid as 'replacement levels'. This issue receives particular attention in some of the debates about alternative pension types, where a distinction is made between defined benefit schemes for which pensions are calculated using a formula that takes into account previous income over the working life or in the period immediately before retirement (or some more complicated combination of those two) and defined contribution schemes where it is amounts paid in that determine benefits (although not necessarily in any simple way). We return to this topic in the next chapter.

Comparisons of replacement levels are, however, very complicated. A description of how my pension relates to past income illustrates this. The UK university teachers' scheme works with a formula that provides anyone who achieves 40 years in the scheme a pension of half their final gross pay plus a lump sum. The latter immediately adds a complication since to compute the real value of the pension, account needs to be taken of the value of the lump sum if annuitised. That term is used to describe a process used to convert a lump sum into an income flow. Insurance companies do this using estimates of their returns from investing a lump sum and predictions of life expectancy. Since annuities vary in what they provide, it is hard to be precise, but it is probably the case that one of these would make the value of a full pension around 60%–65% of previous gross earnings. Translating this into a net value equivalent then requires taking into account taxation, which will tend to fall more than proportionately on a fall in income since less will be taxed at the higher rate. What people actually get, however, will (a) obviously be affected by earnings level before retirement and (b) tend to be less than 50% of earnings since few reach 40 years in pensionable service. If former university teachers are over pension age then they also have the state pension; this (broadly speaking a flat-rate pension although pensioners may have some small earnings-related addition) adds further to the actual replacement rate achieved but in a way that will have a greater impact upon the replacement rate of those with lower pre-retirement incomes. A final complication is that the pension rates applicable to this example are uprated annually – generally in line with price inflation. If, then, a replacement rate calculation is to be done, should it take as the earnings starting point the level at retirement, that level similarly increased in line with the movement of prices or a comparison with what a pensioner might have been expected to be earning at the later date if they had not retired?

You see in the last paragraph a number of complications about computing replacement rates applying to members of one particular defined benefit pension scheme. If you ask me to calculate my own replacement rate I could do so, with difficulty and with a range of possible answers according to the assumptions used. To work out, however, what is the average replacement rate for university teachers in the UK would be a difficult calculation and the dispersion around the average would be so considerable that there would be good grounds for regarding that average as fairly meaningless.

Inasmuch as there are many different arrangements for different occupational groups, comparison of replacements rates is difficult. The example I have been able to use comes from a scheme using a comparatively simple defined benefit formula. Defined contribution formulae obviously yield results that, except in retrospect, make comparison impossible. In much of the debate about pensions attention focuses upon the value of public pensions relative to earnings. In international comparisons, then, a more or less flat-rate scheme like that of the UK offers a replacement rate that changes dramatically according to the levels of earnings used as a reference point, while schemes that are graduated in relation to earnings change less (although many work with guaranteed minima, which have an impact on the replacement rate at the bottom of the earnings range).

If we look at ways of calculating the replacement rate in respect of the comparatively simple UK state pension arrangements we see that there is still room for several perspectives on the replacement rate. In April 2005 average gross earnings for men were £471 a week and for women £372. At the same time the basic state pension was £82.05 for an individual and £131.20 for a couple. However, the guaranteed minimum pension credit (see pages 34–5 for a discussion of this) was £109.45 for an individual and £167.05 for a couple. Table 3.1 suggests some alternative replacement rates based on these figures. The lower the income the more likely the pension credit can be secured. Hence, the comparisons of the pension credit with earnings of half the national average suggest that the state pension for a couple offers a reasonably high replacement rate for families with only one low-paid worker. The higher you go up the income scale the more it is evident that an income source other than the state pension is vital to secure a reasonable replacement rate.

Table 3.2 compares the UK situation with state pension replacement rates in other countries. Given the complexities of this subject already uncovered here it is recommended that these figures are treated as pretty rough estimates, subject to great variation according to the assumptions built in. It is noteworthy that the UK figures in Table 3.2 are above those computed for Table 3.1. The figures provided by the Organisation for Economic Co-operation and Development (OECD) are actually predictions based upon the pension rules applying in 2002, for all mandatory pensions whether public or private based upon full working life assumptions. In the UK case this means that assumptions are made taking into account both the basic state pension and the State Second Pension (disregarded in Table 3.1), together with (where applicable) pension credit. In addition, the reference point for the replacement rates in the OECD study is the average industrial wage, hence the actual figure used for the UK was below that used in Table 3.1. Despite these reservations, this source shows how replacement rates tend to be higher for people

---

Table 3.1: Estimated replacement rates in the UK, April 2005 (%, rounded to nearest whole number)

	Replacement rate where earnings were half the male average	Replacement rate where a man earned half the male average and his wife half the female average (total £421.50)	Replacement rate where earnings were equal to the male average	Replacement rate where earnings were twice the male average
Single flat-rate pension	35	–	18	9
Flat-rate pension for a couple	56	31	28	14
Pension credit for a single person	42	–	23	12
Pension credit for a couple	71	40	35	18

Table 3.2: Net replacement rates of public pension schemes in various countries

	Replacement rate where earnings were half the average (%)	Replacement rate where earnings were equal to the average (%)	Replacement rate where earnings were twice the average (%)	Ratio between low-income and higher-income replacement rates
Australia	77	52	37	2.1
France	98	69	59	1.7
Germany	62	71	67	0.9
Japan	80	59	44	1.8
Netherlands	83	84	84	1.0
New Zealand	77	40	22	3.5
Sweden	90	68	74	1.2
UK	78	47	30	2.6
US	61	51	39	1.6

Source: OECD (2005a, table 4.2, p 52)

with lower earnings and highlights the significant difference between countries where the state scheme offers high replacement rates right up to twice the median income (notably the Netherlands, Sweden and Germany) and those where replacement rates fall quite sharply (as in the UK) as earnings rise, making the contributions of private pensions important for higher earners.

This section has thus shown that the UK state pension system (along with those in a number of comparable countries – Australia, New Zealand and the US) offers comparatively poor replacement rates, particularly for workers at or above the median income level. However, it has also been suggested that there are many problems about trying to evaluate pension arrangements in terms of their replacement rates.

Inclusiveness and pensioner poverty

As already noted, while the issues about the inclusiveness of pension schemes can to some extent be considered separately from the issues about replacement rates, the two topics are closely interconnected. What particularly connects them is that judgements about the current or future adequacy of pension arrangements need to be considered in terms of the extent to which they prevent poverty among pensioners. What is meant by poverty – a topic much disputed in both political and academic arenas – must, as far as pensions are concerned, be judged in terms of the absence of sufficient income replacement in old age. While in evaluating any specific pension scheme the level of income replacement it offers is an important consideration, in evaluating the functioning of national pension arrangements as a whole this must – as is already apparent from the discussion in the last section – be in terms of the extent to which such income replacement as occurs lifts everyone up to an adequate level of income (with adequacy something that is generally explored in terms of some sort of concept of poverty line). This interconnectedness is emphasised by the fact that many systems of income maintenance for older people, including, in particular, the

UK one, are nowadays designed to prevent anyone falling below a defined income level. In other words, many countries have special arrangements (a first tier, see the further discussion of this in the next chapter) to deal with the gaps that may exist within mainstream pension arrangements.

Much of this discussion will therefore be about the extent of low income (pragmatically speaking 'poverty', since I have no intention of being drawn deeply into the arguments about how exactly poverty should be defined) in retirement. It is self-evidently easier to focus upon the issues about the incomes of those who are already retired than to explore issues about potential problems for future pensioners; hence, this discussion deals with that, while a later section examines attempts to estimate the extent of future problems.

It needs to be recognised that the current situation may not offer a good basis for the prediction of future problems. In the UK pensioner incomes have been steadily increasing in recent times. This amelioration needs to be seen as primarily a product of the fact that an increasing proportion of people are entering retirement with good pension provisions. While this is to a large extent a product of past efforts to improve pension arrangements it is also affected by the fact that large numbers are retiring from employment situations in which it has been possible to contribute to private pensions. Our situations in retirement are reflections of our previous incomes. The high dependence of income in retirement upon income before retirement means that this favourable trend is reversible if earning opportunities fall. Indeed, the facts that the UK experienced high unemployment between the mid-1970s and the mid-1990s, that there have been substantial downward pressures upon wages (particularly at the bottom end of the wage distribution) and that inequality has significantly increased since the 1970s have all had long-run effects upon retirement incomes. These have increased the need for attention to the pension arrangements for low-income workers, undermining the assumptions of those who saw the rise of private pensions to be something that would continue steadily.

The UK government publishes regular analyses of the income of pensioners (National Statistics, 2005). As noted above, these show substantial recent growth in pensioners' incomes, at rates faster than other incomes. The mean net income of pensioner couples was £345 in 2003-04 and of single pensioners £181. An important feature of the overall average income figures is that only 42% of the gross income of pensioner couples and 61% of the gross income of single pensioners comes from state pensions and benefits. In the case of the couples, 30% of this income comes from occupational and personal pensions, and 23% in the case of single people. The report from which these figures come notes the growth in money from private occupational pensions as the fastest growing element in the growth of pensioner incomes.

At the very centre of issues about pension reform are questions about the relative roles of public and private pensions in the provision of pensioners' incomes. Table 3.3 shows the dispersion of income, and brings out particularly clearly the division in the system between dependence on state benefits at the bottom end of the income distribution and the role of private pensions (and other income) at the top end. In the middle of the distribution – on account of the diminishing role of means-tested support – the importance of state benefits diminishes in absolute as well as obviously in relative terms.

Viewing this data in terms of questions about inequality and poverty, the key points must be (a) that it is increasingly inappropriate

Table 3.3: Weekly incomes of pensioner couples in the UK, 2003-04, by quintiles

	0-19%	20-39%	40-59%	60-79%	80-100%	Mean
Gross income	£185	£247	£308	£410	£924	£388
State benefits	£151	£181	£190	£189	£169	£170
State benefits (%)	81	73	62	46	20	44
Private pensions (%)	12	22	30	40	41	33
Other income (%)	7	5	8	14	39	23

Source: National Statistics (2005, table 19, p 51)

to assume that pensioners are generally poor, but (b) that it is important to bear in mind the continued presence of a poor group within the pensioner population as a whole.

The upward trend in pensioner incomes is evident from another of the differences within the group that needs noting: on average, younger pensioners have higher incomes than older pensioners and this difference is principally explained by differences in the significance of private pensions as an occupational source. However, it also needs to be borne in mind that the relative value of pensions tends to decline with age. State pensions (and public sector employees' private pensions) are uprated, but in line with prices, not wages. Many other private pensions are not uprated at all.

Another key difference within the group is that female pensioners have lower incomes than male pensioners, with again less from private sources. We return to this later in the chapter.

The National Statistics (2005) report on pensioners' incomes provides a breakdown showing the dispersion around the average by dividing the surveyed population into quintiles. Table 3.4 reports some of this evidence.

Clearly some yardsticks are needed for judging these figures. One possible one is to use the official 'state' minimum enshrined in the benefit level for pension credit. The figures quoted earlier in this chapter are for 2005, their equivalents for 2004 were £160.95 for a couple and £105.45 for a single person. The average for the bottom 20% of the population was close to that. There is a possible problem here about the treatment of housing costs, since there is a means-

Table 3.4: Distribution of pensioner incomes: median incomes for each quintile (before housing costs) in the UK, 2003-04 (£s)

	Bottom fifth	Next fifth	Middle fifth	Next fifth	Top fifth	Overall mean
Couples	169	222	272	349	546	345
Single persons	95	129	129	193	278	181

Source: National Statistics (2005, table 17, p 47)

tested benefit providing some support for rent payers. However, that should mean that in fact no rent payer around that average should have any housing costs. However, the statistical tables also quote 'after housing costs' averages that are lower: £150 and £77 for this quintile. Hence, what we seem to have here is evidence of serious poverty even when it is defined in terms of the official minimum.

Poverty lines are sometimes defined in terms of incomes below either 50% or 60% of the median income. In this case it would not be appropriate to use the pensioner median but rather the wider population figure. Some figures for average wages were used earlier in this chapter. There the male mean wage in 2005 was quoted as £471. The overall mean income for single pensioners quoted above is 30% of that and that for couples is 59% of it. But, apart from the differences of dates, this is not a very satisfactory way of making the comparison since there are specific techniques used for official calculations that take account of differences in household composition to assess both the median income and those falling below it in a more satisfactory way. Table 3.5 uses some data from European Union comparative studies of income distribution to offer some figures for the UK and for other countries with which it may be compared. Interestingly, this suggests a not dissimilar conclusion on the extent of poverty to that suggested by the estimate using the pension credit minimum.

The question this obviously raises is whether either of these figures should be used as criteria for judging numbers with unsatisfactory pension arrangements. Since, as shown in Chapter Two, the pension credit level guarantees an income well above the basic state pension the key question for the UK is about the extent to which the important differences to explore from the policy point of view concern the divergence between those who do and those who do not derive significant income from private pension schemes. We are then drawing a distinction between the 82% of pensioner couples and 59% of single pensioners who do have this source of income and the rest (National Statistics, 2005, table 15, p 43). These figures seem rather high, leading to speculation as to whether this sample is biased towards the better off. However, it should be recognised that

Table 3.5: Percentages of the over 65s in the European Union with incomes below 60% of the median equivalised income compared with the whole population below that level, 2001

Country	Over 65s	Whole population
Austria	24	12
Belgium	26	13
Denmark	24	10
Finland	23	11
France	19	15
Germany	12	12
Greece	33	20
Ireland	44	21
Italy	17	19
Netherlands	4	11
Portugal	30	20
Spain	22	19
Sweden	16	9
UK	24	17

Source: European Commission (2004, p 188)

some of these beneficiaries will have very small amounts of private pensions (unfortunately the data source does not answer this question).

Poverty, means-tests and pensioners' costs

This leads us on to questions about what the future holds for UK pensioners if the system remains unchanged; these are discussed in a later section.

There is, however, another issue about pension adequacy that needs some consideration. Inasmuch as pensioners' incomes are close to the poverty line, problems arise about extra costs for individuals and families. There are several particularly important issues here – about housing costs, about fuel costs and about health and care costs – but brief attention must also be given to a variety of other situations in which pensioners are often deemed to need extra help to meet costs or are able to pay lower charges for items. Furthermore, inasmuch as the solutions chosen for these problems involve means-tests they create extra complications that may interact with pension issues.

On housing, it is interesting to note that the Pensions Commission gave considerable attention to the issues about owner-occupied housing as an additional asset, mitigating some of the concerns about pensioners' income, but no attention to housing as a cost. While it is true that owner-occupied housing, once mortgages are fully paid off, is a realisable asset for individuals and that the passing on of these houses on death is a source of resources for many families, its maintenance may still impose costs. The UK system deals with this issue by making some allowance within the pension credit calculation for these costs, adding here, then, yet another item on which income from pension credit may diverge from that provided by the basic state pension and the State Second Pension. But bigger complications arise in respect of rent payments, which do not affect pension credit but for which another means-tested benefit — Housing Benefit — is available. Another means-tested benefit is available to both owner-occupiers and rent payers in respect of another cost, which, while not exactly a housing cost, is appropriate to mention here — Council Tax. These benefits are available as separate deals to low-income pensioners who do not receive pension credit, but problems arise from the fact that people do not know about or want to seek these entitlements. The overall issue is, then, that these extra ways in which pensioner incomes are de facto enhanced are unambiguous. They do not operate, then, as outright entitlements, yet are a potential source of disincentives to pre-pension-age saving and other forms of self-help.

Another issue of concern to people on low incomes is fuel costs. As fuel prices rise, these form a rising proportion of the costs to be met by people with low incomes. There are particular concerns about the fuel costs of pensioners. Many older pensioners are likely to be sedentary and may well face health problems. A problem of hypothermia has been identified, where people who aim to make savings in their heating bills may be, as they age, increasingly physically unaware of their actual heating needs. Over the years there have been various attempts to tackle this issue via means-testing, none of them satisfactory. In recent times the government has resorted to an alternative, a once-a-year fuel cost supplement for all pensioners regardless of income. While I would not wish to advocate the means-tested alternative I cannot help wondering, as I note this addition to my own more than adequate income, whether the administrative costs of this are justified. Surely the best option is neither this special addition nor means-tested additions but overall pensioner incomes at a level where such special help is unnecessary.

A related but more complex issue arises over health and social care costs (I take these together since they are closely linked). Essentially, mainstream healthcare (I exclude here some issues about dentistry and eye care) is free in the UK for all older people and children (and largely free, except for prescription costs, for all adults). There is a more serious issue about social care. The crucial anomaly in the UK health and social care system is that, while hospital care is in all respects free, social care is not. The issues about this are outside the scope of this book. However, there is one issue relevant to a discussion of pensions inasmuch as charges for social care may be reduced and the normal way of doing this (indeed the statutorily required way as far as residential care is concerned) is by way of means-testing. Since a high proportion of the recipients of social care are pensioners, we thus have yet another way in which the actual welfare of pensioners will be determined by means-tests, and accordingly another way in which inconsistencies of the kind already noted in relation to means-testing may arise. The picture is, then, further complicated by the existence of a variety of other benefits to support care costs to which various entitlement rules apply, generally not involving means-testing. Across the whole area of health and social care for older people it is appropriate to raise questions of principle, and identify anomalies, around the issues about the extent to which what is at stake is the special needs of people who are old or who are disabled or whether it is the extent to which they have low incomes that make it impossible for them to pay for themselves.

This leads me to close this section by mentioning, as indicated in the introductory remarks, that the examples noted here by no means exhaust the range of special provisions to reduce costs for older people. There are many ways in which public authorities and even private organisations subsidise older people. I have already questioned why I should receive a payment towards my fuel costs. There is also in fact a ludicrous pensioners' Christmas bonus of £25 that some past government thought an attractive vote-buying wheeze and no subsequent government has had the courage to repeal. I could equally ask why I should be entitled to cheaper travel, lower-cost admission to museums, cinemas, sports facilities and other places of entertainment and so on. In some cases these concessions may make business sense – helping to fill up cinemas in the afternoons – but in many cases they flow from the general image of the 'poor' pensioner. Again I do not advocate the means-tested alternative; various studies have indicated how unsatisfactory it is to have multiple means-testing, often applying different and even conflicting principles. But I do question the extent to which the notion of the pensioner as a poor person needing a variety of special subsidies hinders the achievement of satisfactory incomes for all pensioners.

Adequacy in the future

The analysis so far has shown that there is considerable pensioner poverty in the UK but that there have been steady improvements over the past few years, so that in many respects incidence of poverty is correlated with age (although it must not be forgotten that that association is also a consequence of the tendency of women – who are less well provided for – to outlive men. We return to this below.) The Pensions Commission (2005, p 42), however, suggests that the 'current pensioner income is at an historic high relative to average earnings' and goes on to explore why this situation will probably not last. Its reasons for pessimism about the future involve assumptions about both the state system and the private system. The analysis in the last section suggests that there is a distinct divide between those with and those without private provisions. Hence, a good starting point for this discussion is the evidence on the extent to which future pensioners will benefit from good private arrangements. We can then go on from that to the rather more complex issues about the extent to which public schemes currently compensate those not covered in this way.

The Pensions Commission (2005, p 50) has published a complex tree diagram showing that out of the working-age population 41% do not contribute to a private pension. That percentage is made up of 34% who do not contribute even though they are in employment and 7% who are economically inactive. The Commission has also identified within the group not covered by private pensions 3.9 million people (an additional 11% of the total working-age population) whose partners contribute to a private pension. It is obviously impossible to guess the extent to which these people have pension rights embedded within schemes to which partners belong, or will be adequately protected by their partner's pensions. We will return later to some of the issues about pension coverage for women, as, of course, most of this group will be female. However, even the most optimistic view of this scenario suggests that half the working-age population are not participating in private pension schemes.

A dimension that this approach does not do justice to is the differences between different types of employment. Public sector employees are better protected in that they are much more likely to be in adequate schemes. This is important for the large number of low-paid employees in the public sector, and for the significant role of that sector as an employer of women. That is a point that has an implication for efforts by the government to shrink the size of the public sector and to contract out activities (often, indeed, low-paid activities – social care, cleaning, catering and so on) to the private sector.

It is important to bear in mind that contributing to a pension is a long-term matter. Therefore a static picture of numbers contributing to private pensions at any point in time does not convey a very satisfactory picture of sustained contributing over time. An optimistic view might be that many of the non-contributors will become contributors, perhaps they are young or only temporarily non-contributors. A pessimistic view, on the other hand, would suggest that many contributors may not sustain their contributions sufficiently to acquire an adequate pension. There is already extensive evidence of lapsing of personal pension contributions.

Then a further complication is that what really matters is *both* sustained contribution records *and* relatively large contributions. Some of those recorded as contributing may be making such low payments each month that they will not secure adequate pensions in the long run. What exactly this means depends upon the pension scheme. While the relationship between contributions and pensions is quite explicit in the case of defined contribution pension schemes, some individuals may be in defined benefit schemes where cross-subsidies within the fund compensate for relatively low contributions at least during parts of individual careers. It is also the case that employers' contributions (another complication when estimating pension adequacy) are much more likely and generous in defined benefit schemes. In relation to this issue it is important to note the significant decline in defined benefit schemes.

In the context of UK policy the rules relating to the pension credit scheme are pertinent here. Poorly financed private pensions may not lift individuals significantly above the income threshold guaranteed by the state. This means that these people will have made sacrifices to pay contributions during their working lives that have little or no impact upon their income once retired.

Various attempts have been made to forecast inadequate pension coverage taking all these complications into account. Obviously this is easier to do in respect of people near the end of their working lives than early on in them since there is more past behaviour to take into account and less future behaviour to predict. The Pensions Commission suggests that around 60% of 50- to 65-year-olds may be on target for pensions above the adequacy benchmark the Commission uses. The Commission's efforts to go beyond this involve a lot of bold assumptions about employment participation and savings.

The Pensions Commission does, however, leave little doubt that radical changes in behaviour, of a kind that it is unreasonable to expect of many low earners and insecure workers, would be necessary to generate a level of private pension provision that would bring everyone over the pension credit threshold. The crucial point here concerns the percentages of incomes that would need to be put into pension contributions to secure adequate private pensions. We get here into some difficult issues about the predictive modelling of behaviour. The Pensions Commission did some work on this; it is not appropriate to quote from it here in any more detail. The Commission argues:

> There exists a segment of the market, people of around and below average earnings, working in small and medium firms or self-employed, to which a freely competitive market cannot now, and will not in future, deliver pensions ... simultaneously high enough to make the segment profitable for the financial services industry, and low enough to deliver good value to savers. (Pensions Commission, 2005, p 126)

Moving on to the questions about adequacy of the state scheme it is possible to make estimates of the numbers whose incomes from the compulsory state schemes – the basic state pension plus the state second pension – will fall below the minimum guaranteed by the pension credit. However, given the combination of the fact that the first two are index linked to prices but the government has taken a more generous view of pension credit, the answer to that question will be a very high proportion of the pensioner population. Hence, one logical answer to the question as to whether there are gaps in the UK state system is 'no', because the means-tested system is available to all. In that sense there is no need, in the UK as opposed to other countries where the means-tested safety net is less adequate, to be concerned about what impact low earned income or periods outside the labour force have upon pensions. On the other hand, as was pointed out in the analysis of the incomes of actual pensioners, there is – and is likely to continue to be – underclaiming of the pension credit. However, it is appropriate to be concerned about a state contributory scheme that increasingly delivers an inadequate income relative to any yardstick, including the state's own minimum guaranteed level. Quite aside from any argument about the desirability of means-testing there must be concern that a contributory system, imposing costs and diminishing net income during working life, will – for many – deliver an income less than that guaranteed even if no contributions had ever been made. If no effort is made to remedy this situation it would at least be honest for the government to acknowledge that National Insurance contributions are merely a form of taxation.

Gender issues

In the UK, and doubtless in many other countries, it is women who are particularly likely to be in poverty in the later years of life. Arber and Ginn (2004) show that three-quarters of those receiving the means-tested pension credit in 2001 were women, almost all of them not (or no longer) married. Since the benefit would normally be paid to a man if there were a marriage, the remaining quarter of recipients would mostly have been couples, implying even more women indirectly dependent on this benefit. This female poverty thus needs to be seen as a function of factors operative during the pre-retirement years and factors related to the period in retirement. The former are:

• inferior labour force participation opportunities in general;
• the impact of expectations that the burden of caring (particularly child care but other forms of care as well) will fall upon women; and
• insecure partnership arrangements between men and women, which increase the likelihood that this caring will occur outside marriage.

The latter are linked to greater longevity, with two implications:

- that pensions tend to decline in value over time; and
- where economic security came from dependence upon a man, widowhood may well largely terminate that.

The extent to which pension arrangements in the UK address these issues needs to be explored in terms of the considerable importance of private pension arrangements and in terms of the extent to which the state pension scheme addresses these issues, but the interaction between the two is also important.

The simple forms of private pensions, with benefits entirely dependent upon contributions, are in principle gender blind: anyone may purchase one. In practice, of course, possession of these assets reflects inequalities in income, wealth and employment. That means that it is males who are much more likely to enjoy the benefits of these schemes than females. The growth of female employment has corrected this bias, but only to a limited degree. In the context of the remarks above on the extent to which, in the UK, the key link to good pension income is private scheme participation, the prospects for women do not look good.

There are three issues here: levels of employment (including the extent of part-time employment), levels of income and the extent of broken periods of employment. Table 3.6 provides some statistics on this, enabling the UK situation to be seen in the context of the European Union as a whole.

While some care is needed in using statistics of this kind, because of the problems of definition involved (see Hantrais, 2004, pp 74-91), they do show that throughout the European Union women are less likely than men to be employed, and when they are employed they are likely to earn less. This is essentially, however, a 'snapshot' view, offering little evidence on female working lives as a whole and thus on the issue of broken patterns of employment.

As a snapshot, moreover, it does not enable us to recognise the fact that there has been a strong recent growth in female employment,

Table 3.6: Some indices of female employment in the European Union

Country	Female employment rate 2000	Female rate as % of the male rate	% of female workforce working part time, 2000	Full-time female pay as % of male pay, 1999
Austria	60.1	78	28.3	79
Belgium	50.3	74	40.5	89
Denmark	72.0	90	43.1	86
Finland	65.4	92	17.0	81
France	56.1	80	30.8	88
Germany	58.8	81	37.9	86
Greece	40.9	58	7.8	87
Ireland	55.0	72	30.1	78
Italy	41.1	60	16.5	91
Netherlands	65.2	79	70.4	79
Portugal	61.1	79	16.3	95
Spain	41.9	59	16.9	86
Sweden	70.4	96	36.0	83
UK	65.1	83	44.6	78

Sources: European Commission (2003, 2004)

with the obvious consequence that many women in the later years of their working lives are much less favourably placed in respect of the cumulation of pension entitlements than *we assume* younger women will be. The expression *we assume* is emphasised here – while there are grounds for optimism, no trend like that should be taken for granted.

The data in Table 3.6 suggest that in looking at the UK in its European context there is considerable scope for increasing female labour market participation and women's wages. It brings out in particular the importance of part-time work for women, a pattern of employment that does not lead on to high pensions wherever these are contribution linked.

Arber and Ginn's (2004) analysis of General Household Survey data shows that while the differentials in receipt of private pension income between men and women apply to all marital statuses except single status, even in this case the median amounts women were receiving in 2001 were much lower than what men of this status were receiving. In the case of the divorced and separated, 57% of men were receiving private pensions but only 36% of women.

For women who are able to join private pension schemes the use of formulae that relate pension to final pay and length of employment doubly disadvantages those, including above all women, with shorter careers. This doubling occurs because of the extent to which short careers also diminish the opportunities to reach the highest terminal incomes.

A particular additional problem concerns the career that is terminated early. Developments to make pensions of this kind 'portable', enabling transfer of rights between employment, or 'freezable', so that entitlements may be accessed long after leaving that employment, help with, but do not entirely eliminate, the disadvantages that flow from early exit from a specific defined benefit pension scheme.

In respect of the state public pension systems there have been some efforts to address gender biases. There are two issues here (reflecting the alternative approaches to pensions policy already discussed): the operation of the rules relating to social insurance pensions, and the ways in which means-tests are used. In respect of both the distinction that has been made by Sainsbury (1996), and others, between the male breadwinner model and the individual model of social provision is relevant. But the two issues will be discussed separately here.

Within marriage the extent to which females benefit from pensions acquired by males depends almost entirely upon private transfers within the family. The extent to which private pensions can be inherited varies considerably. As far as public policy is concerned there have been changes to inheritance and divorce laws that have slightly increased the extent to which women benefit from these pensions. But these must be offset against the very substantial increase in divorce and the high incidence of single parenthood. There are, moreover, grounds for regarding this as a very unsatisfactory device in the context of high levels of cohabitation outside marriage and high levels of marriage break-up early within marriage (making long-run protection for divorced people difficult to make fully effective).

The salience of the male breadwinner model is particularly evident in the UK and in many of the other pioneering European social insurance schemes. These schemes were devised at a time when female labour market participation was low and the standard assumption was that men were the 'breadwinners' while female work (I use that word deliberately) would, after marriage, be confined to the home and family (the housewife 'married to the house', as feminists have mocked).

It is instructive to look at how Beveridge (1942) dealt with the issue of women's position when he made his recommendations that were so influential for the shape of the British social insurance scheme. Beveridge was critical of the way the earlier insurance schemes dealt with benefits for married women and he condemned the Census for including married women 'who do not work for money outside their homes among unoccupied persons'. Nevertheless, in his plan he adopted an approach to provisions for married women, which quickly dated (if they were not out of date already). The reasoning used by Beveridge was set out in a quotation in Chapter Two (see page 27) and in the discussion that followed it.

While Beveridge's use of the concept of a 'team' in his view of married life has perhaps (for its time) an egalitarian ring it must be recognised that such language was also used to mark distinctly unequal relationships. In the labour market of Beveridge's era women did not necessarily choose to be non-participants, they were often firmly excluded from competition with men.

It was noted in Chapter Two that later reforms phased out the special option enabling married women to pay lower contributions. However, on the benefit side the 'two can live more cheaply than one' assumption was not abolished. Moreover, to accommodate the differential impact of that reform the social insurance pension rules prevent a couple drawing both a pension at the 'team' rate and an additional single person pension, a provision that in effect devalues the contributions made by the woman.

There is, of course, a case to be made for Beveridge's model as recognising a basis for the provision of a pension for a wife, if only as a dependant. Sainsbury (1996) contrasts the continued operation of this principle in the UK and the US with the use of a purely individual rights model in the Netherlands and Sweden. This has the consequence in the Netherlands, where female labour market participation remained low for a long while (and is still largely part time), of leaving many women without any kind of pension. If the modern pattern (at least in Europe) is taken to be typically female labour participation but with many withdrawing from full-time participation in the labour force for periods during their life when they undertake child care (or, of course, adult care in some circumstances) then the issue is one about the extent to which insurance schemes can include rules to credit in missing contributions or compensate for low ones if employment is part time. It should be interposed here that compensation for time spent on caring duties is seen conventionally as an issue about protecting women, but can equally apply to men. National systems have moved some way down this road, with the Scandinavians in the lead. The UK's progress has been in fits and starts, with a female social security minister (Barbara Castle) advancing in this direction in the 1970s and a government led by a female Prime Minister (Margaret Thatcher) making cuts that eliminated some of the gain.

In the UK the rules about the impact of time out of the workforce upon the basic state pension and the State Second Pension are complex. The Pensions Commission, in its first report (2004), describes the presence of a number of 'cliff-edges' penalising people who have spent a lot of time out of the workforce in complex ways.

Where pensions depend upon means-testing, the issue, discussed above, about the 'two can live more cheaply than one' assumption surfaces again but the more serious problem concerns the way means are calculated. The pensions guarantee is not an individual guarantee, it involves a means-test in which couples are assessed as a single unit. Governments have generally been unwilling to concede the case for a pension for one member of a couple when a partner has resources sufficient to lift them both over the defined need threshold. It is understandable that they should baulk at the cost implications of moving to individual means-tests but the consequence is discrimination much more against women than men. Many women as a significant group of people who tend to accumulate lower basic state pensions (and are less likely to be in good private schemes) do not benefit from pension credit as individuals since their spouses' incomes are also taken into account. This has been specified here as a women's issue but it can, of course, operate the other way round, with male pensioners being unable to secure pension credit on account of their wives' incomes, although this is a less frequent occurrence. Interestingly, amidst all the celebration about the possibility of gay marriage, little attention was paid to the implications of the application of this aspect of the means-testing of couples.

There is an area of female advantage in our society – greater longevity in general – that is also a source of disadvantage as far as pensions (particularly private pensions) are concerned. Table 3.7 compares the incomes of single pensioners by gender. It shows female

Table 3.7: Average incomes of single males and females contrasted, UK data, 2003-04

	Single males under 75	Single females under 75	Single males over 75	Single females over 75
Gross income	£265	£214	£225	£184
% of that from benefit income	48	58	56	71

Source: National Statistics (2005, table 5, p 23)

disadvantage in general, both in terms of lower income and higher dependence on state benefits, and it shows how this increases with age. While the crude figures suggest a high income fall for males on ageing, by £40, contrasted with a fall of only £30 for females, if you look at these as percentage falls they are similar – 15% and 14% respectively. The crucial difference between older and younger pensioners is in the extent of dependence on state benefits. These mitigate the impact of the increasing absence of private income sources. This demonstrates again the importance of the public system for women.

While few now argue for a return to the model of marriage that Beveridge worked with, it is nevertheless important to recognise that shifts towards defined contribution and privatised approaches to pension issues do require attention to be given to gender differences both in terms of the factors that influence individual incomes and in terms of longevity. Within state systems, credits to deal with periods of time undertaking caring responsibilities have been given widespread attention. There is no evidence of a similar level of attention to this in respect of private pensions; indeed, logically this could not occur unless either schemes allowed for distinct cross-subsidies or public money was put in to perform a compensatory function. A research article on the consequences of the pension mix for Dutch and Danish women, in two societies where there are quite strong first-tier pension arrangements that are under threat, explores this issue and ends up pointing out how much overall 'the normative aim of the pension mix ... is still focused on men's income, rather than ... on individuals and their individualised rights'. It goes on, therefore, to say: 'As long as labour markets, wages, pension schemes and last but not least, care are gender differentiated, the concept of individualisation, based on the principle of equality, does not fulfil its promises' (Fredericks et al, 2006, p 489).

In the absence of this the fact that many households comprise couples (of course, irrespective of gender, although it is female disadvantage that is the main focus here) in which roles may be divided so that one is a much higher earner than the other cannot simply be disregarded. In such a context, then, issues about inheritance of pensions (as opposed simply to state benefits for survivors) surely need to be addressed much more.

It may be concluded, then, that, given role divisions within households (use Beveridge's 'team' expression if you wish), a largely individualist rhetoric about pensions, with a strong emphasis upon private pensions, will contribute to continuing inadequate provision for many.

Conclusions

This chapter has explored the complex subject of pension adequacy, stressing its multiple dimensions. In the context of the politics of pensions it cannot be expected that pension reform will deal solely with issues about adequacy in terms of concerns about poverty and the exclusion of certain groups from benefits. Contributors will have views, which they can be expected to press strongly, about returns for their contributions and about income replacement. Systems need to balance the alternative principles for judging adequacy. However, there is a need to give attention to the extent to which there is in the UK a distinct division between those whose incomes in old age depend very largely on private pensions and those who depend upon the state. While it may be Leftist utopianism to expect that substantial private advantages will be abandoned, it is Rightist utopianism to expect that a system can be devised in which private pensions operate satisfactorily right across the income distribution.

4

Alternative pension models

Introduction

The debates about the UK pension system have become increasingly informed by comparisons with other systems and by a worldwide debate about the most appropriate system for the future in an increasingly global economic system. This chapter therefore looks at the alternative approaches to pension provision.

The Organisation for Economic Co-operation and Development (OECD) has adopted an approach to the classification of pension systems in terms of the notion of tiers. This facilitates discussion of the alternative ideologies outlined in Chapter One, the concern to operate pension systems as deferred wages and the concern to provide an adequate income for all.

The OECD defines systems in terms of the presence of:

- a first tier offering universal coverage and providing a redistributive element inasmuch as a concern to prevent people falling below a basic minimum has a redistributive effect;
- a mandatory second tier using an insurance approach, which may be either defined benefit or defined contribution based, may be funded or 'pay-as-you-go' and may be either publicly or privately provided;
- an optional private third tier.

This approach uses a number of concepts that need to be explored further. Hence, the initial discussion in this chapter will be divided into some considerations about the characteristics of the first two tiers.

The first tier

The OECD shows that the first tier (universally present in the nations belonging to the OECD) has the following variations for mandatory public pensions:

- social assistance (involving a separate means-tested scheme);
- basic (flat-rate pensions unaffected by other income);
- targeted (pensions paying a higher benefit to poorer pensioners and then tapering off for the better off);
- minimum (like targeted but based upon rules within the second-tier scheme).

There are three crucial issues here, which such a classification leads us towards but does not fully explore:

- whether the minimum is available to all;
- where the minimum is located (that is, what level of income is guaranteed);
- the extent to which effects that may deter self-provision are embedded in the system (here the 'basic' pension idea stands out as avoiding this while the others probably do not).

The issue about availability to all concerns what is to be done about those who have contributed little to the second-tier pension schemes that are available. The most simple, but most radical, way of dealing with this problem is to operate first-tier pensions without any contributory rules. Such an approach involves simply making old age (defined in terms of being beyond a specified age) as the sole qualifying condition and funding payments out of taxation. This is often described as the 'citizens pension' approach, on the assumption that some concept of citizenship would be the qualifying condition, to prevent an influx of older people from other societies. It may also be noted here that where systems have diverged far from their original contributory bases, so that citizens perceive insurance contributions as simply another kind of tax (as in the case of the UK), a further decisive step in that direction might be logical (I return to this in Chapter Eight).

Writing non-contributors into pension arrangements may both be costly and have some tendency to undermine any contributory principles that are operated for second-tier schemes. Many schemes have special arrangements to deal with sickness and unemployment and, sometimes, spells taken out of the workforce because of parental responsibilities and other caring duties (issues about this were discussed in relation to pensions for women in Chapter Three). But then what about people who have:

- never tried to enter the labour force;
- evaded payment of contributions;
- spent much of their lives in prison;
- lived abroad, or migrated from another country;
- been so disabled that they have never been able to enter the labour force?

The above list was deliberately set out in an order that is likely to correspond with conventional views of 'deservingness'. The first two items particularly highlight the dominant notion of pensions as a reward for consistent participation in the normal labour market. That notion is then modified to various degrees by a recognition that people should not necessarily be penalised if they have been unable to do this, with unemployed people, sick people and carers as the main candidates for this. At the boundary – and people obviously take different views about where that boundary should be – however, there is clearly a problem if, despite rules about contributions, many people secure pensions who were not, but could have been, contributors. Crucial here is the question already raised about what is meant by 'work' in this context.

The OECD distinction between the tiers is based upon the notion that two tiers – one non-contributory, one contributory – can exist side by side. This implies that a relationship between them can be established that prevents those effects in the list above that are regarded as undesirable. Crucial here, of course, is the relationship between the level of benefit guaranteed for the first tier and that customarily expected for the second. Some of the issues about this were explored in Chapter Three, where replacement rates were compared. Systems with high minimum guarantees relative to the benefits provided by second-tier systems stand out as providing better replacement rates for people with lower than for those with higher incomes.

However, the issue here is about more than just the levels of income guaranteed, it is also about rules that govern access to the two tiers. To avoid the criticism that first-tier schemes indiscriminately undermine social insurance, the crucial 'gate-keeping' device has been the means-test (which after all was what social assistance schemes used to ration benefits before social insurance was invented). Hence, in many systems we see means-tested pensions operated to supplement insurance pensions. It has been shown in Chapter Two that in the UK's system we see means-testing operating, contrary to Beveridge's expectation that it would diminish in importance as the social insurance system matured, as an increasing aspect of the system.

Means-testing brings with it another set of problems. In relation to benefits for older people in the modern world (much more than in the early days of pension schemes) means-tests need to give attention to assets as well as income. Older people are likely to have significant amounts of savings and may have choices between simply retaining assets and transmuting them into income streams. Means-testing of assets is, then, further complicated by the various forms assets may take, including owner-occupied housing, and by the ways ownership of assets may be easily shifted to others (notably children). Inasmuch as the last-named possibility leads to Inheritance Tax being described as an avoidable tax, so too may the means-testing of assets be avoidable. We see evidence of this problem in the UK in respect of the means-test used to determine state contributions to residential care for older people.

But there is perhaps an even greater problem than this, which emerges inasmuch as governments encourage private forms of pension provision. This is that the presence of an underlying but means-tested guarantee of assistance in old age can inhibit contributions to private alternatives. This is particularly pertinent at the margins – where relatively low-income individuals can only 'save' for their old age at serious cost to their current standard of living. Aspects of this were discussed in the last chapter.

Arguably this is particularly a UK problem, because of the particular emphasis in government policy (described in Chapter Two) upon strengthening the safety net while disregarding the social insurance pension. However, the problem occurs in more subtle forms in some other systems. In Sweden, for example (see the further discussion below), there is an integrated pension scheme with both elaborate contributory rules and a guaranteed minimum, with the consequence that people whose contribution records give them entitlements close to the guaranteed minimum will in effect derive proportionately less benefit from their contributions.

The second tier

The OECD's second tier can be seen to be diverse and classifiable in terms of two dimensions, which come together in different ways in different countries. This is presented in Figure 4.1. The definition of

Figure 4.1: The OECD's dimensions for analysis of the second tier

	Public	Mixed	Private
Defined contribution			
Notional accounts			
Defined benefit			

the second tier set out on p 71 contained several expressions that need to be explored further at this stage:

- the distinction between funded and 'pay-as-you-go' schemes;
- the distinction between defined benefit and defined contribution arrangements; and
- the notion that these schemes may be either publicly or privately provided.

These are issues that are in practice tangled together quite complicatedly. This discussion will aim to bring out the key issues. Its starting point is a book by the World Bank (1994), which has been both influential and controversial. Where the OECD talks about 'tiers', the World Bank talks about 'pillars', but these are essentially the same. The World Bank argues that direct public provision should be limited to the first tier (or pillar) and that the second should be funded and mandatory, but privately managed. Figure 4.2 sets out the World Bank's recommended model.

Figure 4.2: The World Bank's pension pillars

	(1) Mandatory publicly managed pillar	(2) Mandatory privately managed pillar	(3) Voluntary pillar
Objectives	Redistribution and co-insurance	Savings and co-insurance	Savings plus co-insurance
Focus	Means-tested or minimum flat rate	Personal or occupational savings plan	Personal or occupational savings plan
Financing	Tax-financed	Regulated and fully funded	Fully funded

Source: Adapted from World Bank (2004, figure 3, p 15)

The World Bank's report is a work of policy advocacy, the pillars are what they would like to see, not what there is on the ground in the world. The report itself acknowledges:

> Most countries ... combine all three functions in a dominant public pillar, a publicly managed scheme that pays an earnings-related defined benefit and is financed out of payroll taxes on a pay-as-you-go basis. People with high incomes contribute more and get more, but some of their contributions are supposedly transferred to people with lower incomes. This combination of functions has been defended on grounds that it keeps administrative costs low through economies of scale and scope and that it builds political support for the plan. The savings component encourages high-wage earners to participate, whereas the redistributive component lets them express their solidarity with those less well-off. In industrial countries, these plans have been credited with reducing old age poverty during the post-World War II period. (World Bank, 2004, p 12)

In addition, another variation on the World Bank model involves either accompanying a dominant state social insurance model with a state-regulated investment scheme (see the discussion below of the Swedish development) or operating a state-controlled compulsory savings scheme (see the discussion of provident funds in Singapore below). Another modification of the World Bank model that could be introduced into this discussion is a further version of pillar two from which the word 'mandatory' is replaced by something like 'strongly encouraged' (we will see this as a feature of UK policy proposals in Chapter Eight).

Public versus private, funding versus pay-as-you-go

It is appropriate, then, to explore some of the ideas embedded in the arguments for and against the World Bank's approach, to highlight some of the key issues in the contemporary pension policy debate. This will be done by drawing first some public–private contrasts and then moving on to the implications of obscuring these.

The early pension schemes developed by states to reward their ex-employees involved simply the use of money collected through taxation from the public. It was rare for private employers to be willing to commit themselves in the same way; they turned instead to various ways of securing savings from employees towards pensions, often seeking the support of insurance companies to run such schemes. When states then developed schemes to extend beyond their own employees they often drew upon these private models.

Private pensions come in many forms; it is not proposed to get bogged down here in all the variations. The simplest form of purely private pension involves an agreement between a contributing individual and a pension provider that is no more than an undertaking to invest savings and repay them in some form (this may be as an annuity; see Glossary) after the end of employment or at a defined age. What the individual gets out is then a product of what was put in plus whatever that money earned while it was invested. Of course, then, as the standard warning about investment says, 'the value of these may go down as well as up'. These are 'defined contribution' pensions, as what the individual gets out depends (other things being equal) upon what was put in.

However, this simple defined contribution approach may be modified inasmuch as a pension provider offers guarantees of growth or inflation proofing that go beyond this simple dependence on the market. What may happen here is that contributions go into a managed pool of investments, which spreads the risk for any individual.

Where employers are involved in the provision of private pensions they may modify the principle of defined contributions by making advance commitments about what individuals may take out when they retire; in that sense they offer instead 'defined benefits'. To offer defined benefits is to take a risk, in any situation in which there is nevertheless investment of contributions in a fund, that ultimately pay-out obligations will exceed the resources of the fund. In the event of bankruptcy the potential or actual pensioners will have a claim on the remaining assets, which have to compete with those of other creditors. Within the world of private pensions, defined benefit schemes are largely confined to large and strong enterprises. In a capitalist world of rapid organisational change, commitments to pay out defined benefits are seen as increasingly problematical. There is clear evidence that they are in sharp decline in the UK, outside the public sector.

This leads us to the issue that there may be problems if defined contribution schemes, let alone defined benefit ones, are directly linked to the economic success of the employer who is offering them. An alternative approach to funding preferred today, and often enforced by government regulation, involves the investment of pension contributions wholly or partly outside the employing enterprise.

A related issue here concerns the impact of pension arrangements that are specifically linked to one employer (and to some extent also one occupation) upon people who move between employments. In the early days of private pension provisions such arrangements could impose heavy losses on those who changed jobs, and gave employers a hold upon employees. There has been a gradual evolution of regulation (and self-regulation in some cases) to limit this problem, enabling accumulated pension assets to be 'frozen' until later or to be 'portable', that is, transferable to other schemes. But losses still occur, in various forms depending upon the scheme rules and individual circumstances.

This approach to pension provision brings into play a variety of intermediary organisations that manage pension funds, claiming to ensure that the growth in value of invested contributions is at least as good as the growth of the economy as a whole. Decisions need to be made about how to invest the money, and therefore also when a movement from one investment to another is appropriate. What is involved here are 'portfolios' in which money is invested in a number of different institutions. There are questions to be addressed about appropriate levels of 'risk' for investment. The safest investments tend to yield lower returns than the more risky ones. Fund managers need to trade off through mixtures of investments the need for security and the desirability of high returns, moving money between these in response to changes in the market. Fund managers expect to be well rewarded for these activities. Hence, it costs money to manage a pension fund. The returns that individuals get from their invested pensions funds will be reduced by such administrative charges.

However, the issue of administrative charges can add up to much more than the costs of fund management. If the organisations managing pension funds are independent of both the state and the employers and in competition with each other then selling their services to employers and employees, and dealing with the ensuing collection arrangements, will involve administrative costs. Indeed, the more independent these organisations are the greater may be those costs. There is thus another trade-off problem here inasmuch as the advantages of competition to pensioners need to be offset against these administrative costs.

This discussion could proceed here into 'deep water', exploring the traditional pro-capitalist arguments that efficiency is maximised through competition with some of the alternative anti-capitalist concerns that large and powerful organisations are able to transfer costs to the public in ways that are hard to monitor or control. Clearly, choices between private and public approaches to pension provision are influenced by views on this topic. It is not appropriate to go into this here but it is important to bear in mind that the administrative costs of private pension schemes are often high and that there is a problematical inverse trade off between the amount invested and the impact of those costs on the value of the investment. Administrative costs will tend to have a disproportionate effect upon small pensions, and particularly pensions invested for a relatively short time. The whole topic is, then, further complicated by the fact that difficulties in selling pensions to, or administering arrangements with, economically insecure groups (including here small employers) will push up administrative costs. These issues arise particularly in respect of the more individualised approaches to funding; the maintenance of a large collective fund for a group of people facilitates the sharing of the administrative cost burden.

Administrative costs may thus make private pensions a poor deal for low earners or people with varied circumstances across their working life. One solution here, which, for example, will be found in the various UK policy proposals to promote private pensions, is for the state to seek to regulate administrative costs or (as in one of the Pension Commission's proposals) to be an intermediary to reduce those costs. But since such interventions themselves impose market distortions, the administrative costs problem may alternatively be seen as an argument against state support of the private road to pension provision.

So far, then, we have arrived at a definition of pension 'funding' (or, as some say, 'pre-funding') from the point of view of the private sector. In the words of the glossary in the first report of the Pensions Commission, funded pension schemes are ones 'in which pension contributions are paid into a fund which is invested and pensions are paid out of this pot' (Pensions Commission, 2004, p 295).

Governments may encourage private pension provision through tax subsidies. Principally this is likely to take the form of tax relief upon contributions into pension funds. One rationale for this may be that private pensions will ultimately be taxed, when individuals receive the pension, although this may be at a time tax liability is lower. Not surprisingly, the existence of tax subsidies provides another rationale for government regulation of private pension schemes.

There may also be forms of tax relief on the payment of pensions too, perhaps taking the form of lower rates or higher allowances applicable to persons over pension age. There may also be more complicated tax subsidies relating to profits earned during the lives of pension funds.

When governments set up pension schemes they have to make a series of choices about how they will operate (bearing in mind the concepts that are applied to private arrangements). They have to decide:

- Will the pensions they provide be 'defined benefit' or 'defined contribution' ones?

- If 'defined benefit', how will that principle operate – in relation to need, or to contributions or to past incomes and so on?
- If 'defined contribution', what modifications will they make to the simple operation of that principle (to take into account differences in the capacity to contribute)?
- If they decide to collect contributions will they put these into a 'fund', and then how will they manage that fund, bearing in mind that it may make a substantial contribution to public investments?
- How will they involve the private sector in the operation of publicly mandated pensions: as the operators of the public system, as sources of supplementary pensions and so on?

Many governments operate state pension schemes without 'funding' or with only limited funding. The alternative to funding is described as 'pay-as-you-go' (PAYG). The Pensions Commission's glossary defines a PAYG pension system as one 'where the pension is paid out of current revenue and no funds are accumulated to pay future pensions' (2004, p 295). However, there is in practice a great deal of confusion about the extent to which, when governments claim to practise funding, they are really doing that. Some very confusing statements are made in many countries about current or expected pension fund solvency, particularly in the US but not in the UK, where the government long ago abandoned any pretence to be maintaining a 'fund'.

This issue of what funding really means in relation to government pension schemes also applied to unregulated private schemes in the early days of private pension provision where funds were not insulated from the general accounts of a company. The key question with regard to governments is: what do they do with the pension contributions they collect? If they were to follow private sector best practice, as indeed generally imposed by them upon that sector through regulation, they would invest the money in forms in which it was separated from general government resources. But that is a rather difficult notion if applied to a government that is engaged continuously in spending and investment. Maybe we would like our pension contributions to be invested in hospitals or schools or roads. But in that case this is what generally happens with a PAYG scheme if it has a surplus of pension contributions over current commitments. Whatever the government may enter into the account books of the pension funds, it uses this surplus income for current purposes. In this sense a contribution to a PAYG scheme may alternatively be seen as:

- a tax payment 'unhypothecated' (that is, not linked to any specific expenditure objective) inasmuch as it enters into general government funds; or
- a direct contribution from current contributors to the incomes of current pensioners.

Exactly which of these descriptions is most appropriate depends to some extent upon the way in which the pension system is managed (that is, how explicitly this relationship is spelt out to contributors) and to some extent on the form – within any nation – taken by conventional discourse about state income and expenditure. Much of the time the UK government is happy to see National Insurance contributions as an unhypothecated tax, only adopting the other stance when it wants to remind the public about rising social security costs. In other countries (France and Germany, for example) the maintenance of free-standing management arrangements for state pension funds, with participation from employers and employers' organisations, keeps alive the notion of an independent account. In these cases it is what we may call the 'bookkeeping' arrangements that are crucial, as far as the protection of individual contributors are concerned. These may be accompanied by actuarial adjustments that take into account how any accumulated fund might grow in value. Nevertheless, it is still true that such schemes are PAYG, inasmuch as assets are merely book entries.

The alternative to PAYG for a government is to do exactly what good private pension schemes do – invest it in productive activities that will protect and perhaps increase the value of these funds for the time they are needed. This, however, generates a situation in which government-controlled pension funds acquire shares in (or other forms of claims upon) private economic activities. This may, however, be seen as covert nationalisation. Blackburn (2002, pp 74-6) shows that when the US developed a contributory pension system in the 1930s that aimed to be funded, the government encountered the objection that government investment in the private sector would be a form of backdoor 'socialism'. It does seem to be this that has restrained some governments from going wholeheartedly down the funding road. Instead, at best, as noted above, they maintain accounts that inflate the value of the 'on paper' assets in the so-called fund by a notional rate.

There has nevertheless been a recent tendency for governments to be happy to fund to some extent, particularly investing what the Pensions Commission calls 'buffer funds' (for example, in Norway and Sweden). One feature of this has become investment overseas, where clearly the issue about covert nationalisation does not arise.

At the same time it is important to bear in mind that in respect of this issue, the public–private dichotomy is not necessarily as strong as it appears at first glance. Pension funds often invest quite substantially in government bonds and other securities, seeing these as providing stable and predictable elements in a portfolio of investments.

This section has sought to set out in reasonably straightforward terms – and without trying to make a case for or against the various options – some of the issues about ways to operate second-tier systems. The pros and cons of funding and PAYG, and of public and private approaches, will be explored further in Chapter Seven.

Trying to classify systems

It is possible to classify nations in terms of the two tiers as identified by the OECD. But in doing so it is important to consider the relationship between the two. Hence no attempt was made to put the names of nations into Figure 4.1. However, Table 4.1 extracts from OECD tables a number of nations and shows how they figure in respect of both the first and second tier. The OECD's elaborate classification has been simplified in the following ways:

- to make the simple distinction between 'basic' first-tier pensions and the use of means- or income-tests for the rest. It may be noted here that the UK is classified as a combination of the two by the OECD because of the presence of the National Insurance-based flat-rate pension as well as the minimum income guarantee, while it seems to me that it is wrong to see the former as a basic pension;

Table 4.1: Pensions systems in OECD countries according to the OECD two-tier classification system

Country	Use of a basic first tier	Defined contribution/ Defined benefit/ Notional accounts	Public/ private
Australia	No	Defined contribution	Private
Austria	No	Defined benefit	Public
Belgium	No	Defined benefit	Public
Denmark	Yes[a]	Defined contribution	Mixed
France	No	Mixed	Public
Germany	No	Mixed	Public
Italy	No	Notional account	Public
Japan	Yes	Defined benefit	Public
Korea	Yes	Defined benefit	Public
Netherlands	Yes	Defined benefit	Private
New Zealand	Yes	None	
Spain	No	Defined benefit	Public
Sweden	No	Mixed	Mixed
UK	No	Defined benefit	Public
US	No	Defined benefit	Public

[a] Since the OECD designates Denmark like the UK as having a basic and targeted system but that designation has been disputed above, it may be that I would similarly want to question Denmark's designation.
Source: OECD (2005a)

- to use two columns to classify separately the dimensions set out in Figure 4.1.

This classification of the second tier does not deal with one crucial variation across the world: the presence or absence of funding. It may be assumed that public defined benefit systems do not have funding and that private defined contribution ones do. It is not implicit in the use of public notional accounts that there will be actual funding. But then there are also various mixed cases, involving part-funding (a topic to which we will return in Chapter Seven).

Finally, there is an issue that needs to be considered in respect of the third tier. There are variations in its strength, that is the extent to which investment in private pension funds occurs. It is important to bear in mind that this is not just an independent economic fact about nations, governments play important roles in the management both of their economies in general and of private pension arrangements in particular that will influence the environment for private pensions. How the second tier operates influences the options for the third tier. Conversely, a pre-existing strong third tier – as in the UK – may have an impact on the politics of second-tier design. Table 4.2 (on p 90) brings out some of the variations in third-tier strength across the sample of nations considered.

Can you then move from this to types? Some writers have tried to do so, but only with a small sample of nations. Attempts to do it with the whole OECD sample run into great difficulties. There are, however, some features that may be highlighted. Perhaps the clearest is the presence or absence of a basic pension scheme, and the variation that in New Zealand this stands alone as the sole public tier. Second, there is a large group of nations where there are fully public second-tier schemes, and within them there are significant variations in the extent to which they operate on pure defined benefit principles (notable here is the way in which France and Germany mix defined contribution and defined benefit through what the OECD calls 'points systems'). Moreover, the presence of the UK in this group suggests that it is a very broad group since in the UK case defined benefit means flat rated, with some marginal modification on account of the operation of the partly optional State Second Pension (and its predecessors). This raises a crucial question about variation around the defined benefit principle in terms of the extent to which it is related to previous income. Third, there is only one nation in that list that is operating in a way that conforms to the World Bank model – Australia – but two others with mixed systems that have changed in that direction (Sweden and Denmark) and a single case that has a private but defined benefit scheme (the Netherlands). Finally, one country in the list is described as using public notional accounts (Italy), but that is also a part of the 'mixed' schemes of Sweden and France (and some other countries not listed in Table 4.1). Notional accounts are described by Whiteford and Whitehouse (2006, p 86) as ones where:

> Contributions are recorded and they earn a notional interest rate, linked to a macroeconomic variable. At retirement, the accumulated notional capital in each account is converted to a stream of pension payments using a formula based on life expectancy at the time of retirement.

Some of the comments in the last paragraph bring us back to the issue already raised in respect of the first tier – that it is difficult to interpret data about defined benefit rules without information about the income replacement levels being aimed at. Something similar may be said in respect of any ultimate judgement about defined contribution schemes although here there will be questions both about what has to be paid in (and by whom – employers, employees – and with what state support) and what is ultimately paid out (plus investment growth, minus administrative charges, with or without any cross-subsidies).

Drawing statistical contrasts

It is all very well to set out different pension models without reference to what they cost, and to whom, and what they provide in benefits. Ideally this section should include some nice comparative tables on this subject. In fact this will not be done; much of the data is inadequate or misleading. However, this topic will not be entirely avoided; some comparative data are set out below, some was included in Chapter Three and other items will be used at various places later in the book.

The reasons for being wary about quantitative comparisons are as follows:

• Many of the crucial questions concern not so much what is happening now but what will happen in the future. From the point of view of the recipients, some schemes are not yet fully mature while others have recently undergone changes that will diminish the benefits to be received in the future. To forecast the future costs or the future performance of pension schemes, predictions are necessary about demographic futures and about future prospects for employment (which affects the contributions side). Hence, predictions tend to involve complex alternative assumptions.

• In terms of both individual inputs and outputs, pension predictions tend to be different for different people. A crucial variation here concerns the impact of income and contribution differences. Distinctions have been noted in the discussion above between schemes where much attention seems to be given to settling an adequate baseline for all and those where the concern is rather more with securing high levels of income replacement. As noted in Chapter Three, in the assessment of any national scheme what it offers to those outside the labour force, those inside but with low incomes, those with average earned incomes and those with incomes of various multiples of the average will differ.

- There are, then, some important issues about the roles of government. In the comparative literature on pensions much attention has been paid to the current and future costs to the government. But data on this can be very misleading. Pensions are transfer payments where governments take in money in various ways from the non-pensioner population (and even to some extent from the pensioner population) to pay out in pensions. These will be both taxes and social insurance contributions, and it is not necessarily easy to draw a distinction between these two. It is all very well, then, to stress the extent of the pension *burden* on government since this is in fact a charge upon the public as taxpayers and insurance contributors. At the same time the public may have to bear another burden, as makers of compulsory or voluntary pension contributions to private pension schemes. It is only the insidious tendency for government exactions from the population to be defined as 'bad', even if they are for citizens' current or future benefit, that seems to lead to much more attention being paid to these than to other aspects of pension costs. Of course, private contributions may be voluntary where social insurance contributions are compulsory, but even that distinction is eroded by the increasing tendency for governments to make it mandatory for people to contribute to private pensions and at least to encourage such activities and implicitly impose penalties in terms of future disadvantages if they do not do so.

Despite these qualifications, and particularly the warning about the misleading ways in which the public–private distinction is used, it is appropriate to try to draw out that distinction in statistical terms here. Table 4.2 contrasts data on private pension expenditure with government expenditure and shows quite clearly the systems with strong public but weak private provision (Germany, France and Italy), those with developing private but weak public provision (Australia), those where there are significant contributions from both sides (the Netherlands, the UK and the US) and a country where provision is

Table 4.2: Contrasting private and public roles in pension provision

	Private expenditure on pensions as a % of GDP	Pension fund and life assurance assets 2004 as a % of GDP	Government expenditure on pensions 2001 as a % of GDP
Australia	3.3	91.3	4.3
Denmark	0.9	91.7	6.5
France	Close to 0	60.0	11.9
Germany	0.6	31.9	11.2
Italy	Close to 0	22.1	13.8
Japan	3.3	48.2	7.6
Netherlands	3.7	140.4	6.4
New Zealand	Close to 0	15.5	4.9
Sweden	1.9	65.4	7.4
UK	3.4	116.2	8.3
US	3.8	115.0	6.1

Sources: OECD (2005b, table 1; 2005c)

overall very low (New Zealand). Sweden's figures seem surprisingly low, although the level of assets suggests changes are afoot.

Some national cases that illustrate aspects of the variations discussed above

An early draft of this chapter sought to outline a taxonomy of pension systems and then set out in a fuller form examples of each. The discussion above is the product of an exploration of that idea that led me to the view that such an activity would be impossible, or at least would present a very distorted version of reality. Instead, this section discusses some national systems to illustrate the complexities of this topic and to highlight some of the ways national governments have sought to structure their systems. Instead of labelling systems in terms of the categories set out above, the subsections here will just be headed by the names of the nations whose systems are to be examined.

The US

The US has a weak first tier, a second tier that is a good example of a straightforward public defined benefit system popular in many countries and a strong third tier.

A flat-rate, first-tier means-tested pension is available either in the form of a federal scheme or, in certain states, a state-based scheme. I am wary of using simple translations into pounds here (ideally comparisons should be in terms of purchasing powers), but a rough calculation suggests that the guaranteed income level in the federal scheme is much inferior to that in the UK pension credit scheme.

The second tier is a contributory defined benefit scheme originally set up in the 1930s in which contributions need to be accumulated over 40 years in employment to get the maximum and then actual benefits depend upon the application of a formula based upon uprated average earnings over that working life. There is a progressive aspect to this scheme in that lower earning levels attract proportionately higher pensions than higher ones and there is an upper limit to payments.

The scheme is PAYG but (as will also be seen to be the case in Germany) accounting procedures are used that enable the monitoring of the relationship between income and outgoings and predictions of future surpluses or shortfalls. There is a special Treasury account into which contribution income is deposited and to which expenditures are charged. Any balance in the fund earns interest at the government bond rate. The size of this fund has been a long-standing preoccupation in pension politics in the US. Obviously these suggest that in the absence of contribution increases benefits will have to fall if there is no other source of income for the so-called 'fund'. The fund has never been allowed to engage in private sector investment. Nevertheless, at times, particularly after legislation in 1983, it accumulated a surplus, which relieved the fiscal pressure on the overall overspending by the US government. This involved a similar cynicism to that which has led the UK to use National Insurance contribution increases to fund additional health policy.

The debate about the impending alleged bankruptcy of the US fund is important in the context of the continued advocacy, both by the neo-liberals and by those who want to sell private pensions, of the elimination or reduction of the US social security pensions system. At the same time, US governments have been prepared to use various tax subsidy devices to encourage a strong growth of private pensions. About half of the US workforce participates in employer-provided pension schemes.

Germany

In Germany contributions to the social insurance scheme are required of the paid workforce. The expectation is that those who participate in the workforce throughout a normal working life will acquire a pension that operates at a relatively high replacement level in relation to their previous earnings. General accounts of the German system tend to stress that it is one where what you take out depends upon what you put in. This is, however, not true in the strictest sense. There are not individual accounts; rather, contribution rates depend upon income and pension rates upon a set of complex rules about pension points taking into account amounts and years of contributions. It also needs to be noted that contributions have to be made by both employees and employers. Hence, there are redistributive elements embedded in the basic formula. In addition, over the years a variety of modifications have been built into the scheme to compensate individuals for periods of sickness and unemployment and for periods of child-rearing. To do this without moving too far from the insurance principle these additional 'credits' for individuals are tax funded. The relationship between the insurance rules and the provisions relating to additional tax-funded contributions is complex and involves a complex politics, affecting not just pensions but other aspects of social insurance (which in the German case includes health insurance).

An interesting feature of the German scheme is the way in which, while it is de facto PAYG, there is a very strict procedure to calculate the bookkeeping entries on behalf of individual contributors (see the further discussion of this in Chapter Seven). The following comment by a German expert conveys this aspect of the scheme together with the continuing adherence to the insurance principle:

> contributions are special remuneration, not instruments of redistribution in themselves. While taxes are levied without any equivalent benefit being granted, social security contributions are characterized by the fact that the contributor will benefit from them. Contributions are payment for benefits. A contributor can assume that his or her contributions will be in balanced relation to the benefits that will follow at another point in time, since his or her entitlements are subject to constitutional protection.
>
> The direct link between contributions and the amount of pension is a positive signal for insured persons and pensioners. Contributors know every single contribution will play its part in raising their future pension. Contributions are not collected in a fund, but pension entitlements and claims, especially those based on one's own contributions, enjoy the constitutional protection of property rights. (Meurer, 2006, p 115)

This offers a distinct contrast to the UK version of PAYG, in which the underlying insurance relationship has been largely forgotten. It accounts for what, to the eyes of a UK observer, is a rather strange debate about pension reform in Germany in which calculations are made about the future of the scheme, taking into account levels of contributions and expected replacement levels for benefits. Policy changes are, then, adjustments designed to keep these two in a balanced relationship to each other so that the so-called 'fund' will not become bankrupt. As noted above, additions provided from general taxation are included in these calculations, but they are strictly limited to the special provisions for credits.

The German system came under considerable strain as a result of reunification, with the federal commitment to including the citizens of the former East German territories in the social insurance scheme on the same basis as everyone else, engendering an elaborate politics around the issues described in the last paragraph. The government's aim was to try to limit contribution increases, leading it naturally therefore to reduce the replacement rates for future pensions. To offset this development the government encouraged the growth of private pension supplements (never entirely absent in the German system) by tax concessions for contributions to these.

The final point to make about the German system is to reiterate the fact that the scheme is employment related, with obvious consequences for those not in the workforce. The benefits are, as shown, contribution and income replacement related, hence, commitments to 'dependants' are not taken into account. From the point of view of women, therefore, pension entitlement depends upon employment participation, except that in modern times credit systems have been developed to cater for periods engaged in child-rearing (three years per child). In addition to women there will be others who fail to acquire adequate contribution records. The German system does include a quite separate means-tested 'safety-net' social assistance scheme for those not covered by social insurance.

The German system can be seen as a good example of a system in which PAYG social insurance is dominant but it does involve some redistribution, funding principles are honoured in principle if not in practice, some private insurance is present and encouraged by the state and there is an underlying means-tested safety net.

Sweden

The Pensions Commission (2004, appendix D, p 123) defines the Swedish scheme as a 'four pillar' one. In practice three of these four are closely integrated. Its first pillar or tier is a minimum guaranteed benefit scheme under which all citizens are entitled to a basic pension, without recourse to a means-test (and at a level above that offered by the also operative social assistance scheme). This is financed out of the general budget, not out of contributions. There is a basic citizenship test for entitlement. There are, then, rules under which entitlements under the second-tier contributory scheme reduce entitlement to the basic pension. In this respect, then, in contrast to the German system, contributory benefits are not unequivocal rights as they are offset against the basic pension entitlement. Individuals only start to benefit from their contributions when their pension income exceeds the minimum guarantee (this is why the OECD classifies the Swedish first tier as targeted rather than basic). Hence, inasmuch as the two schemes are taken together the system redistributes towards lower-income people.

The second tier is a contributory one to which employers and employees together pay 16% of earnings. There is also a system of government-paid credits covering absences from the labour force on account of sickness, unemployment and parental leave. Contributions are cumulated in a notional account for each individual, taking into account the average growth of wages. This part of the scheme has much in common with the German system. Notional accounts do not imply funding. While, on the one hand, the Swedish system is not a defined contribution system in the strict sense of being totally dependent upon invested contributions and is subject to adjustment to take into account demographic change, on the other hand, it is not a defined benefit one since pensions are not explicitly linked to previous income. After retirement the accumulated fund is annuitised, taking into account age of retirement, and then indexed to take into account wage growth in the society.

The third tier is an innovation, following on from legislation in

1998. There is over and above the second-tier contribution a compulsory contribution of 2.5% (again split between employer and employee) put into individual-funded accounts. Since this is a fully funded part of the system that has recently been introduced it will be quite a long while before it has any significant impact on the incomes of Swedish pensioners. Individuals are given a choice of private funds into which their money should go, with the system putting their money into a default fund if they do not exercise that choice. The choice of funds is regulated by a government agency, which also supervises their operation. This is thus not funding by the state. Despite the fact that such ideas were on the Swedish agenda for a long time, it does not give the state a means of control over private enterprise. Investments in all the funds, including the default fund, may be made outside Sweden.

The fourth tier in the Swedish system is not simply the equivalent of the World Bank's third pillar, since even this is not entirely voluntary. It is a system of specific occupational pensions covering around 90% of employees, which the Pensions Commission describes as 'semi-mandatory because of national pay bargaining' (2004, appendix D, p 23).

The Netherlands

The system in the Netherlands has essentially two tiers. The first tier was classified above as a basic pension system. It has a simple residence qualification. It provides a pension calculated as 70% of the statutory minimum wage for a single person or 50% of the minimum wage for a couple living together. This restriction to take into account living arrangements is the only glimmer of a means-testing element in the system; it is based upon residency, not on marriage. It is funded from insurance contributions, but these are not imposed on people without earned incomes.

The second tier is de facto voluntary, and is perhaps more appropriately called a third tier. In World Bank terminology this system is in a sense a two-pillar system with the second one missing. In fact over 90% of employees contribute. They do so to a range of schemes linked either to industries or run by separate employers. Nearly all are defined benefit schemes, with pensions calculated on the basis of formulae linking years in employment with levels of remuneration at or near retirement. Most of the big schemes are the product of agreements between employers and the unions.

The Netherlands is thus interesting for two reasons. First, it has a basic pension that is fairly generous (how generous, of course, depends upon the level of the minimum wage – a pension for a single person based upon 70% of the UK minimum wage would be well above the pension credit level), funded by but not based upon contributions and available to all residents. That would surely satisfy the advocates of citizens pensions in the UK. Second, it has a voluntary private second tier, with much wider coverage than that in the UK, which remains widely still defined benefit. Its strength seems to derive from a combination of cautious funding and tight regulation, together with the fact that many of the specific schemes offer wide coverage across large occupational groups rather than being limited to specific organisations. It would be interesting to know whether the defined benefit principle, which is now so under threat in the UK, is running into any difficulties in the Netherlands. An article by two OECD staff members that lists the many recent cuts in national pension systems makes no mention of the Netherlands. It seems curious that the Pensions Commission, which reports all these facts about the Dutch system, did not seem to have made the short trip across the sea to see how they do it.

Australia

Until recently Australia had only a single first-tier pension system operated by the state on a PAYG basis using a means–test and potentially available on a citizenship basis to all who had lived in Australia for 10 years. This system remains but there is now a privately funded second tier, which was introduced in 1992.

The first-tier means–test is sometimes described as an 'affluence test' since all but about 10% of the population secure some pension.

The system works with the guarantee of a minimum income (which, again, applying a rough calculation as I did for the US, seems significantly inferior to the UK's pension credit) but then a high level of disregard of additional income (up to about 70% of average earnings) and a slow tapering-off rate (40%).

The new second tier is a compulsory-funded private pension subsidised by the state through tax relief.

New Zealand

The New Zealand government provides simply a first-tier basic pension. The sole qualifying condition is residency in New Zealand for 10 years (five of which must have been since reaching the age of 60). There is no means-test. Not surprisingly, the level of payments offers an incentive to make additional private provision (although there are no tax concessions for this). As with the Australian minimum, the New Zealand basic pension seems to compare unfavourably to the UK pension credit. The Pensions Commission (2004, appendix D) analysis of pension schemes in other countries put the New Zealand pension at £4,638 for a single person and £7,050 for a married couple in 2002. The UK basic pension was £6,276 for a couple in 2002 and the minimum income guarantee (pension credit) level was £7,790. But as noted earlier, care is needed about these comparisons. It is not clear what methods the Commission used to translate New Zealand dollars into pounds, and purchasing power comparisons are what are really needed. The aim in New Zealand has been to achieve a 65% replacement rate for average income.

Singapore

Singapore has a very limited social assistance scheme forming the first tier of pension provision. Its second tier is a long-established Central Provident Fund. This involves state-administered individual savings accounts. While these involve distinct funds from the perspective of individuals, and there is provision for state enhancements based upon prevailing interest rates, there are still grounds for doubt about whether this scheme can be called 'funded' in the strict sense inasmuch as it is state managed and is not invested except inasmuch as it provides resources for state investment. Here we have a good example of just how ambiguous the notion of funding can be.

From the point of view of the potential beneficiaries the rules are complicated. Contributions are required of both employers and employees and divided between three accounts: Ordinary, Special and Medisave. Only the Special account is reserved specifically for retirement. The function of the Medisave account is evident from its name. As far as the Ordinary account is concerned, withdrawals may be made for other purposes, notably housing and education costs. Hence, when an individual reaches retirement age what will be available will be whatever is in the Special account and any balance in the Ordinary account.

Balances left on death may be inherited. This is an interesting feature, meriting a short digression. In Western pension schemes, while special arrangements often exist to protect widows and child survivors, those arrangements do not extend to other relatives (however dependent upon the economic activities of the deceased pension holder). While there may be many good reasons why this is the case since the alternative is very open-ended commitments, and many private pension schemes are subsidised by employers and by the state, it is important to recognise that the closer we get to the idea that pensions should be simply savings for old age the more likely it is that people will question why early death should simply bring a benefit to the provider or to other more long-lived pensioners and not to the descendants of the deceased. In any examination of alternative ways of providing for the future – particularly in situations of economic and political uncertainty – it will not be surprising if some individuals decide that there are better ways of protecting assets (particularly in property) than in pension investments. I have been made particularly aware of these issues from discussions with people from East Asia where family transfers and protection systems remain very important, financial institutions are not (or are not regarded as) very secure and political futures are uncertain.

It is difficult to assess the contribution the Central Provident Fund is making in Singapore, and will make in the future, to security in old age. The facts that much of the money can be used for other purposes and that balances can be inherited means that it needs to be seen as state support for family saving as opposed to a simple source of pensions. Commentators have expressed doubts about its viability as an approach to pensions. Nevertheless, it provides a model that has attracted wide interest, and one that has recently been emulated in Hong Kong.

In Singapore there are separate pension schemes for public servants and soldiers and, of course, there are other voluntary third-tier schemes.

Conclusions

The Pensions Commission was quoted in Chapter Two as highlighting the peculiarity of the UK. Looked at comparatively here the UK does not seem so peculiar. An account of the features of the UK system was given in Chapter Two. It showed the UK to have a means-tested first tier, a contributory second tier with two products, one a low flat-rate basic pension, the other graduated additions (for those not opting out on the grounds that they are contributing to an adequate third-tier pension), and a voluntary privately run third tier.

The UK is one of many systems without a 'basic' first tier (although it was noted above that those who did the OECD classification do not altogether agree with that view). If reformers want to shift in that direction the Netherlands offers a good example of such an approach, while New Zealand offers an example of the use of this as the sole state contribution to pension policy.

The UK has, according to the OECD, a public defined benefit second tier. Again, a problem about that identification has been noted above. The weaknesses of the UK's second tier (with its dominant element flat rate) are not altogether brought out by simple attempts to compare, but become much more evident when the details of the German or Swedish systems are examined. In this respect it can be seen as clinging on to a very basic version of social insurance, weaker even than that in the US. On the other hand, funding a flat-rate pension with graduated contributions is progressive (meaning here that it effects some redistribution towards poorer people). Contrasting alternative models for a second tier are offered by Germany (still a public scheme running semi-autonomously with more or less what may be seen as defined benefits), Australia going down the private (and obviously defined contribution) road and Sweden adding a small privately funded effort to its defined benefit public scheme.

When we look at third tiers the UK and the US have much in common, offering a distinct separate pension system for the better off. A comparison with the Netherlands is instructive, since the same system in that country is more universal and more likely to offer defined benefits. That represents something that the pension reformers who prefer private solutions would surely like to emulate in the UK. There must be questions about how sustainable the Dutch system is. However, international data on pension investments suggest that the Dutch schemes have particularly high funds (see Table 4.2). It may be that their schemes have followed funding principles much more strictly than some of their British counterparts who gave employers contribution 'holidays' in the days when stock market returns were particularly high.

While there is no suggestion in the UK pensions debate about going down the road followed by Singapore, that scheme has been outlined to indicate that the main ideas on the Western agenda do not exhaust the possibilities. In Singapore the extreme individualism of personal accounts is interestingly linked not with privatisation but with strong state control. There could have also been consideration of Chile here where the individualism runs all through, but with state compulsion, involving personal funds and private control over investment.

The World Bank's case for mandatory private schemes seems only to have been taken really seriously by Australia and the Netherlands (although this case is complex) among the sample of nations examined here (discussion of another key example of this approach – Chile – has been left out as it does not appear in the OECD classification). However, Sweden and Denmark have moved partially in that direction. The important thing about the UK in respect of this is that it already has a very strong voluntary 'third pillar' (as Table 4.2 indicates – also showing that it shares this feature with the US). This might be taken to offer a strong pointer on where it is heading. We will see in Chapter Eight whether this is indeed the case.

5

Pension age and retirement age

Introduction

While, as this chapter will show, there are ways in which policy and behavioural factors contribute to making the retirement age and pension age coincide, it is nevertheless important to recognise the wide range of circumstances in which this is not the case and the policy implications of that fact. It is moreover important to recognise the false way in which these two are equated in popular discourse. For example, I have sometimes been asked by foreigners 'What is your country's official retirement age?' to which an accurate but perhaps rather pedantic answer is that there is not one, and the only 'official' age to which I can refer is the minimum age for the payment of a state pension. More seriously, contemporary discussion of the latter tends to be handled in the newspapers with statements that people are going to be forced to work longer. Of course, that may be the case but the actual impact of any change in the minimum state pension age upon paid work will depend upon the decisions of other pension providers, upon the availability of such work and upon individual choices.

This chapter will therefore sort through some of the considerations about the relationship between pension age and retirement age. It starts by addressing some important questions, which it is important not to lose sight of, about what we mean by retirement. It will then look at the three logical possibilities for the pension age–retirement age relationship:

- that they are the same, considering the factors that make this quite likely;
- that the pension age comes before the retirement age;
- that the retirement age comes before the pension age (bearing in mind, in the context of the mix between public and private pensions, the alternative definitions of these ages).

In the context of contemporary pension policy it is the last scenario that needs to secure the most attention because of its implications for pension costs and pension contributions. The implications of this are thus explored, leading then into the examination in the next chapter of the 'demographic time bomb' thesis, which is closely linked to this topic and to the debate about trying to change behaviour in respect of the retirement age.

What do we mean by retirement?

It is appropriate to start this discussion by considering the meaning of retirement because this has implications for the objectives of pension arrangements. In Chapter One a number of alternative explanations of the reasons why pensions were developed were reviewed. Alternatives considered included:

- Are pensions seen as devices to enable employers to shed unwanted labour, perhaps as a consequence of lowered work performance in workers' declining years, without adverse consequences for those workers?
- Are they just to be seen as rewards for a period in work, probably accumulated by contributions during that period?
- Or are they regarded as designed to enable everyone to enjoy a secure income in their later years, so that they can continue to participate fully in society?

The notion of retirement, a distinct move from employment to non-employment, is clearly embedded in the first of those. In the second, while the connection with employment is still in evidence, pensions are regarded as earned and what the person does after earning them will probably be of no concern of the pension provider. But in the third the connection with paid work is absent, the concern is simply with income provision, in which case other income sources may be taken into account but whether or not the person is formally retired is irrelevant.

But behind these considerations are questions about the meaning of work. Much of the discourse about retirement is concerned with the termination of paid work. But is it satisfactory to see it solely in these terms? There are a number of problems with the adoption of such a perspective. They have been sources of complications throughout the history of pension schemes, and far from disappearing many of them are arising today in new forms; consideration of some of them is very important for ongoing debates about pension policy.

Some of the issues can be more easily handled than others in the context of these debates. These are the ones about the various ways in which people are remunerated for work outside standard employment contracts. It is increasingly recognised that workers in later life may shift from full-time to part-time employment. We may thus speak of forms of semi-retirement to which pension rules may need to adapt. Since many workers are part time for all or much of their lives (this is particularly true of women in many societies) adaptations of pension schemes to cope with this are already on the agenda.

Similarly on the pensions agenda is the treatment of self-employment. In this case the identification of a specific point of retirement may be particularly difficult. Many self-employed people are likely to continue doing some work deep into old age. For the more fortunate (the author is in this category) this may involve incremental adjustment downwards of the contribution of earnings to income. For the less fortunate there may be more abrupt changes to cope with as activities become less and less profitable.

The situation of the self-employed may be affected by the extent to which their incomes depend upon their collaboration with others.

Historically particularly significant here is family enterprise and for some activities, notably farming, transitions towards retirement may involve subtle and complex shifts in roles within a family.

I believe that situations in which individuals can change their roles slowly with advancing years have a great deal to commend them. In that sense, while only a few people are writers or farmers and so on, the issue here is not just about having pension arrangements that are adapted to these special circumstances but about ensuring that the pension arrangements for all do not make it difficult to adopt ways of life in which transition from employment is gradual.

But the discussion so far still treats retirement as a withdrawal, even if gradual and complex, from paid work. The wider problem about this perspective can best be highlighted by considering the contrast, embedded in the discussion of retirement, that is particularly evident wherever male and female roles within the household are sharply distinguished. Retirement for the male is, then, termination of paid work after which he becomes (perhaps) an encumbrance around the house to a wife whose (house)work life remains much the same. Notwithstanding increased female paid employment and rising male domestic participation that stark contrast highlights the need to consider not merely how we think about retirement but also about the ways in which retirement and pension receipt are related to each other. It is worth saying that while concerns about people's inability to do paid work any more lay right at the root of the development of modern pension policy, inability to do housework is seen, at best, as a special issue for the provision (under strictly rationed circumstances) of services or disablement benefits and, at worst, as a problem to be absorbed within the family.

But the notion of a satisfactory transition from paid work involves more than private arrangements within a household to reconstitute the domestic division of labour since the widely championed notion of an 'active retirement' involves a whole range of voluntary participation (some of it indeed in roles that only differ from other 'employment' in that they are not paid – working in the local hospital or a charity shop or an advice agency and so on). If these activities are important, not just for the welfare of the individuals performing them but also for wider public welfare, then not only do they suggest that the traditional view of retirement should be revised but they also raise questions for pension policy. In the next chapter it will be argued that consideration of what retired people actually do with their lives provides a challenge to notions that pensioners are a burden on society, but here what needs emphasising is that there is a need for incomes sufficient to enable full participation in society.

Retirement and pension receipt as simultaneous occurrences

The discussion in the introduction to this chapter challenged the expectation that retirement age is necessarily determined by the age at which individuals qualify for pensions and the last section went further to challenge the notion that retirement is a simple and readily identifiable phenomenon. However, before going on to explore situations in which retirement age and pension age definitely do not coincide there is a need for a brief discussion of the reasons they often do so. The key to this was offered in the last section: the design of pension arrangements to specifically compensate for the termination of employment. This is, then, given further force in many systems by the use of a specific age at which pensions will be paid. A great deal, then, hinges on the role of the state in determining either retirement age or pension age or, in particular, both together.

Where pensions are entirely private matters, then, the age at which pensions are paid depends entirely upon private actions by employers or negotiations between employers and employees or rules relating to pension schemes. Conventionally, such pensions are paid on retirement from the employment to which they are tied, although in practice there is nothing to stop pension payment being followed by re-hiring and indeed this does occur. However, governments often then impose upon these arrangements laws that limit this freedom of action. They may regulate pension schemes to determine the ages at which pensions may be first paid and to limit re-hiring arrangements. They are particularly likely to do this where they have given tax concessions to pension arrangements (which, of course, then gives them an interest in how their largesse is used). But state interventions into private arrangements may stem from concerns to regulate the labour market: to encourage or discourage the discharge of employees.

In practice, as has been stressed elsewhere in this book, many pension arrangements are hybrid, with both private and public elements. As far as public pensions are concerned, rules about the ages at which pensions may be drawn are more or less universal (there is a grey area of exceptions to this in provisions for severely disabled people but these are generally not seen as pensions). These rules, then, may be seen as having an influence on retirement age if they require termination of paid employment as a qualifying condition.

National differences on the age at which public pension entitlements start are interesting. The use of the age of 65 as the crucial threshold for this is very widespread, but there are some variations between countries, as Table 5.1 shows. In some countries

Table 5.1: Pension ages

	Men	Women
Below 60	Taiwan, Turkey	Taiwan, Turkey
60	France	Austria, Canada, France Poland, UK[a]
62	Hungary	Hungary[a]
64		Switzerland
65	Australia, Austria, Belgium, Canada, Finland, Germany, Greece, Italy, Japan, Netherlands, New Zealand, Poland, Portugal, Spain, Sweden, Switzerland, UK	Australia, Belgium,[a] Finland, Germany, Greece, Italy, Japan, Netherlands, New Zealand, Portugal, Spain, Sweden
66	Ireland	Ireland
67	Denmark, Norway, US	Denmark, Norway, US

[a] These countries have enacted measures to bring the female retirement age up to the male one.

---

the age at which labour market withdrawal seems to be encouraged is much earlier than in others. France is interesting as a country where the pension age was explicitly lowered to 60 in 1983. This may be seen as a response to high employment, encouraging older workers to leave the workforce. However, it has been described in a history of modern France as 'the most enduring improvement to the quality of life' at that time (Kedward, 2006, p 486). This is an interesting point of view, contrasting sharply with an alternative view that the French government made a costly mistake.

It may also be noted that there are a number of countries in which there is a male–female differential that is quite low and that it is being eliminated in several other countries (see note to Table 5.1). An odd trio of Austria, Canada and Poland are the only countries in that list where quite large differences remain.

The promise of a pension may be seen as a strong 'pull' factor inasmuch as the worker is otherwise turning down a payment for which there is no need to work. But that, of course, is often not so straightforward. The case for giving up employment for a benefit will depend upon the level of that benefit. Moreover, real-world pension arrangements do not usually pose the dilemma in quite so stark a form. There are likely to be rules relating to deferred pensions – about how they may be uprated, about whether they may be enhanced by further contributions – which any worker offered the chance to continue working will want to take into account. There may also be other considerations relating to the tax treatment of pensions and/or earned income after the official retirement age.

Those are comments about the 'pull' side of the equation, but then there are often 'push' factors to take into account. These have, in the UK and much of Europe until very recently, tended to operate strongly in the direction of forcing the coincidence of pension age and retirement age by enabling employers to require retirement ages to correspond with pension qualification ages. This is all beginning to change with the enactment of measures to prohibit age discrimination. This will not entirely give choices to workers because the legislation that is beginning to emerge includes concessions to employers' concerns about the work capacities of older people. These take the form of provisions to enable them to carry out tests of competence. However, the shift away from taking specified retirement ages for granted is a feature of the contemporary concern with demographic change to be discussed in the next chapter.

Employment beyond pension age

In this section, as in the last, any discussion of working beyond pension age has to take into account the fact that, while state systems tend to work with one fixed pension age, private systems may (subject, as noted above, to state regulation) work with a variety of different age points. As a consequence of private pension arrangements there are significant groups of people in many societies who considered themselves to be 'retired' long before the state retirement age. In the UK there are two crucial thresholds, one of them being age 50 (this will become 55 in 2010) because of regulations that prevent most pensions being paid before that date and the other being age 60 because that has long been used as the standard retirement age for many public servants. These are now very much under attack from the government. So we have a significant group of people who may be considered as 'early retirees' in public policy terms but as late retirees inasmuch as they have continued working beyond the date at which their pension became available. Many of them will be able to combine employment with private pension receipt.

However, the concern of this section is not with those who are in employment beyond the date at which they become entitled to a private pension but with those people who continue in employment beyond the state pension age. There are some interesting data about this group in the UK, deriving from Census data. Macnicol (2006, p 84) notes that 'The proportion of males aged 65+ defined in each census as economically active has fallen steadily each decade ... from 73.4 per cent in 1881 to 7.5 per cent in 2001'. There has been an upturn since 2001 but only a small one. So the phenomenon of the employment of males beyond state pension age has become rare in the UK. The position with regard to females has been more complicated. The existence of an early state pension age of 60 for females (soon to be phased out) has been used as a device to push women out of the workforce earlier. This has been successfully challenged in the courts by women who have been adversely affected by this, limiting their number of years in private pension schemes and forcing them out when they still have a lot to offer.

In relation to these phenomena, questions about 'pull' and 'push' must be considered. Clearly, in looking at the massive change that occurred until the 1970s, the pull of improved pension arrangements must have been important. But on the other hand – as will be evident when we examine pre-pension age departure from the workforce in the next section – there must be some consideration here of the lack of availability of employment.

This massive change in post-pension-age working by males, then, needs to be considered against a context of higher health standards and rising life length expectations. There are two alternative ways of looking at this:

- as a change to be reversed, perhaps by changes to the pension qualifying age;
- as another reason to be concerned to ensure, through appropriate pension policies, that the social – as opposed to economic – participation of older people is addressed.

These issues will be left there for the time being, to be explored later in both the next chapter and the examination of policy options in Chapter Eight.

Retirement before pension age

In looking at retirement before pension age there is a need to return to the question of what is meant by retirement. In this section the concern is, of course, with retirement from the workforce. But even then we may identify alternative ways of looking at this. Surely many an employment adviser will have reacted angrily to someone reluctant to seek employment, asserting that they seem to have decided to retire at a very early age (perhaps even before effectively entering the workforce). However, Census and Labour Force Survey questions have little difficulty in making a distinction between those who explicitly say they have retired from the labour force, who are largely people who have secured private pensions before the state retirement age, and others. Within those others they use ways to distinguish between those who are unemployed and those who are not actively seeking employment.

What, then, is more difficult is to satisfactorily distinguish, from those not actively seeking employment, those who may be said to be discouraged workers who have drawn the conclusion that they have no chance of getting employment. Particularly problematic here is the fact that within this group will be many people with ill health and disabilities.

Finally, there is within the group of people outside the labour force people (mainly female) whose non-participation is attributable to domestic and caring duties. Even this phenomenon is more ambiguous than perhaps it once was. In a context of rising female labour market participation, choice as to whether or not to be in this group may be affected by employment opportunities. Even governments have changed their treatment of women in this group in some circumstances; hence, the UK government has given attention to trying to enhance the workforce participation of childless wives of unemployed men.

All this adds up to a very complex situation in respect of people towards the later years of the conventional working life who are outside the labour force, some of whom straightforwardly consider themselves as retired (and mostly do not bother the official system because they live on private pensions) and a large group of people who may be defined as de facto retired from employment even if they and/or governments are reluctant to accept that this is the case.

The rising cost of the support of the latter group (when set alongside also rising pension costs and the fact that they will mostly not be pension fund contributors) set against a background of assumptions (as discussed above) about the improved health of older people has put concern about them very much on government agendas as necessarily a part of the pension policy agenda. The rest of this section examines the data on this phenomenon.

Table 5.2 uses OECD labour force statistics to analyse employment rates of males aged between 55 and 64. Alongside data for 2000, figures for 1970 have been added (from those countries for which data are available). The contrast between these two years shows how much less common early withdrawal from the labour force was in 1970. There are some remarkably low employment rates listed for 2000, particularly in Finland, France and Italy. In every case for which data are available these rates are below those of 1970.

Table 5.2: Employment rates of males aged 55-64, 2000 and 1970

Country	2000	1970
Canada	58	79
Finland	44	73
France	38	74
Germany	48	79
Italy	30	48
Japan	78	85
Netherlands	50	79
Norway	73	83
Spain	55	83
Sweden	68	84
UK	60	[a]
US	66	81

[a] The source does not include a figure for the UK in 1970; it does give 62 for 1990. There was probably no comparable Labour Force Survey in the UK in 1970; my estimate from 1971 Census figures is an employment rate of around 85%.

Source: Casey et al (2003, table 7, p 40)

The Pensions Commission's first report contained a useful analysis of the composition of the group of people who had left the labour force before the age at which they would qualify for the state pension. It notes that 'only 53% of women remain in employment by age 59 and only 42% of men are employed at 64…. The average age of exit from the labour market for those men who were economically active at 50 is now 63.8' (Pensions Commission, 2004, p 34).

The Pensions Commission goes on from this to try to separate out the influences upon early retirement, by examining income groups of men aged over 50 divided into quintiles. While about 50% of men in the lowest quintile are not in employment, less than 5% say they are retired. By contrast, a much lower proportion of the richest quintile (25%) are not in employment but nearly all of them say they are retired. The Pensions Commission (2004, p 34) says that 'a large percentage of the people in the lowest two quintiles described themselves as sick or unemployed, while most of the richest quintiles of earners who have left the labour force described themselves as retired'.

Such data highlight the extent to which early withdrawal from the labour force is often a matter of personal choice for the well off but rarely so for poorer people. Faced by the growth in this group the UK and other governments have come to the conclusion that attention should be given to increasing the labour force participation of many of these individuals. After a period in which – as a response to unemployment often designed to mask its severity – governments were willing to tolerate labour force withdrawal by older workers, enabling them to be categorised as disabled or even (as, for example, in the case of France) allowing forms of official early retirement (Kohli et al, 1991), the growth of this group has come to be seen as a policy problem. Nevertheless, it will take a big rise in employment to bring the levels up to those of the middle of the last century (see Table 5.3). Moreover, the earlier trend (with a significant fall in labour force participation as unemployment increased in the 1970s and 1980s) suggests that this reversal may be as much a function of rising employment overall as of changing behaviour by older people. The

Table 5.3: Average age of exit from the workforce in the UK

	Men	Women
1950	67.2	63.9
1960	66.2	62.7
1970	65.4	62.4
1980	64.6	62.0
1990	63.5	60.9
2000	63.3	61.1
2005	64.0	61.9

Source: Pensions Commission (2005, figure 1.44, p 97)

UK government is giving considerable attention to reducing the ranks of those drawing long-term sickness and disability benefits but this is so far making little impact upon the size of the group of older claimants.

Conclusions

The primary aim of this chapter is to stress the need to understand that the relationship between pension age and retirement age is a complex one, with the two often diverging from each other. Pension arrangements inevitably have an impact upon retirement decisions; however, it is not necessarily the case that changes to the age at which pension entitlements begin will significantly affect retirement decisions. There is a need to look at the many factors that are driving people out of or attracting them into the labour force. This is an issue to be explored later in Chapter Eight in relation to proposals for policy change. It is equally fallacious to see retirement age decisions as simply matters of lifestyle choice, as implied by cheerful bits of journalism that proclaim that the increasingly healthy young elderly are choosing increasing leisure. That option is open only to those who have strong private pension entitlements at a relatively early age.

The issues about retirement age are strongly bracketed in discussions of pension policy reform with demographic data about the rise of the older population relative to the younger population (the demographic time bomb scenario). This suggests, among other things, a need for public policies that will postpone retirement. This chapter has indicated that doing that may be difficult. Issues about workforce participation may be important for policy but these need putting in a wider context. The next chapter will take up that theme but will go further to cast doubt about many aspects of the demographic time bomb thesis inasmuch as they start with a set of simplistic assumptions about older people as in a sense parasitical upon younger people.

6

The alleged 'demographic time bomb'

Introduction

The predicted impact of demographic change is an important influence upon pension policy. Many of the statements about this are alarmist, writing of a 'demographic time bomb'. This chapter will take a cool look at this, not denying the basic demographic evidence but questioning how that is interpreted.

It will be shown that it is certainly true that in all developed countries, and even in less well-developed countries outside the area where the scourge of Aids is intense, the numbers of older people are growing and will certainly continue to grow. The result is, in the context of a low birth rate, a change in the ratio of older people to prime-age adults. However, there is a need to address the following questions:

- Do the figures on the relationship between the numbers of old and the numbers of younger adults provide a realistic picture of the extent of 'dependency' now or in the future?
- Is the dependent–non-dependent relationship within a nation determined by demography or by economics or indeed neither?
- What in any case is meant by 'dependent'?

Beyond the last of these questions are wider, largely philosophical, debating points about the extent to which a growth in the numbers of so-called dependants matters, confronting the strong productivist logic of much conventional thinking. This is largely beyond the concerns of this book, nevertheless inasmuch as the presence of older people is seen as a problem for societies it colours the whole debate about pension provision.

Having addressed these questions I will not have dismissed the concerns of the 'demographic time bomb' thesis, merely suggested that they tend to be exaggerated. This leads to the next chapter, which considers the conclusions about pension systems that stem from the thesis.

The demographic evidence

Table 6.1 sets out the evidence on the age structure of the UK population at various recent points. This shows how the numbers of those over pension age have grown relative to others. The fact that this occurred against the background of a falling birth rate meant, across the period 1961 to 2001, that the so-called 'dependent' group – the old plus the young – remained much the same. But the long-run implications of the two trends are a substantial growth in that group, consisting increasingly of the old. The further you look ahead, of course, the more inaccurate the predictions will be. But we may assume that death rates (unless there is a war, a massive epidemic or some other major disaster) will remain much the same or even fall a little more. Predictions of birth rates are more uncertain; there could be further changes in reproductive behaviour (earlier predictions

Table 6.1: Percentages of UK population in various age groups, 1961 to 2001

	Under 16	16-64	Over 65
1961	25	63	12
1971	25	62	13
1981	22	63	15
1991	20	64	16
2001	17	63	20

Source: www.statistics.gov.uk

have been falsified by unexpected changes of this kind). Perhaps the biggest unknown as far as future predictions are concerned is in levels of immigration and emigration. There may well be significant increases in the numbers of prime-age adults and children as a consequence of this. Conversely, since the UK is not as yet (global warming could make a difference) seen as a venue for retirement, immigration by significant numbers of older people is unlikely. There will be some emigration of older people, but since most pensions are portable, to the countries to which retirees go, this will have little effect upon the need for pensions. None of these uncertainties refutes the general thesis that the need for pensions for UK citizens will increase while the prime-age adult population will probably fall.

Table 6.2 shows similar data on the growth of the population aged over 65 between 1960 and 2003 in a range of countries for which good comparative statistics are available.

The comparative data show wide variations in the pattern of ageing. There are some, all European, nations with relatively high proportions of older people before 1960; in some of these the increases in those proportions were quite slight between 1960 and 2003. There is also a group with quite low proportions of older people in 1960 that have experienced little change (notably Austria and Belgium). Around the world as a whole the most dramatic changes are in those nations where the proportion of older people has risen very fast from a low starting point in 1960, above all Japan and Korea, but to a lesser extent also some of the southern European nations, together with Finland and Poland.

If changes in countries like the UK have been comparatively slight up to now, the crucial questions for pension policy are about what the future holds. The Government Actuary has produced predictions for the UK, which cannot be exactly compared with the data in Table 6.1 since it uses the age of 14 as the break point for children and the age of 60 as that for older people. These predictions suggest a slight fall in the under 14s but a big growth in the over 60s from about 21% in 2005 to 23% in 2010, 26% in 2020 and 29% in 2030. These figures highlight the impact of the 'baby boom' after the Second

Table 6.2: Numbers of older people in various countries, 1960 and 2003

Country	% over 65 in 1960	% over 65 in 2003	2003 as % of 1960
Australia	8.5	12.8	151
Austria	7.9	8.8	111
Belgium	8.2	9.0	110
Canada	7.6	12.8	168
Czech Republic	9.6	13.9	145
Denmark	10.6	14.9	141
Finland	7.3	15.5	212
France	11.6	16.2	138
Germany	10.8	16.6	154
Greece	8.1	16.8	207
Hungary	9.0	15.3	170
Ireland	10.9	11.1	102
Italy	9.0	18.2	202
Japan	5.7	19.0	333
Korea	2.9	8.3	286
Netherlands	9.0	13.8	153
New Zealand	8.7	11.9	137
Norway	10.9	14.8	136
Poland	5.8	12.9	222
Slovak Republic	8.9	11.5	129
Spain	8.2	16.9	206
Sweden	11.8	17.2	146
Switzerland	10.7	16.0	150
UK	11.7	15.6	133
US	9.2	12.3	134

Source: OECD (2004, pp 6-7)

World War (applying also to many other European countries). This obviously produced initially a big growth in the proportion of the dependent young, then a significant growth in the adult population (although not then with as big a growth in the birth rate as might have been expected given changing patterns of marriage and procreation) and now a big rise in the numbers of older people. While this is a special sequence of events, which will not necessarily be repeated, it is very salient for the contemporary pensions debate.

There are various predictions about the future. These typically look at the growth of the older population relative to the younger population, either comparing the numbers over 65 with all below that age or with the numbers of adults. Table 6.3 cites such a comparison, looking at the ratio of older people to people aged 20-64. Looking at the issue in this relative way highlights the 'dependency ratios' that figure in predictions of the problems associated with these changes. The prediction quoted relates to a date rather far ahead, 2050, and cites figures for almost all the nations featured in Table 6.2.

It is interesting to note that the UK and the other European nations whose populations were already quite old by 1960 tend to be expected to experience less growth in the proportion of the older population in the 50 years after 2000. However, overall these data give no evidence to question the concern about demographic ageing across the developed world.

The Pensions Commission (2004, chapter 1) explored the varied predictions of actual life expectancy in some detail. There is certainly a considerable element of uncertainty in relation to any prediction, although – on the whole – as time goes on the prediction's uncertainties go up. There are still substantial differences in life expectancies between different socioeconomic groups, suggesting that increases in the standard of living (and perhaps reductions in inequality if they occur) will increase the size of the older population. The Pensions Commission also notes survey data that indicate that people tend to underestimate their own life expectancies.

Table 6.3: Estimated ratios of the over 65s to 20- to 64-year-olds, 2000 and 2050

Country	Over 65s: 20-64s 2000	Over 65s: 20-64s 2050	2050 as a % of 2000
Australia	18	40	222
Austria	23	55	239
Belgium	26	42	180
Canada	19	44	232
Czech Republic	20	59	295
Denmark	23	42	183
Finland	22	46	209
France	25	46	184
Germany	24	49	204
Hungary	21	50	238
Ireland	18	40	222
Italy	27	66	244
Japan	25	72	288
Korea	10	55	550
Netherlands	20	42	210
New Zealand	18	38	211
Norway	24	44	183
Poland	18	50	278
Spain	25	68	272
Sweden	27	27	174
Switzerland	24	55	229
UK	24	39	163
US	19	32	168

Source: United Nations (2003)

Do the figures on the relationship between the numbers of old and the numbers of younger adults provide a realistic picture of the extent of 'dependency' now or in the future?

The last section set out the data that are used for the arguments that a problem of increased dependency is arising because of demographic change. This section challenges that perspective as an oversimplification. The most important point to make about the demographic data, and particularly the findings cited in Table 6.3, which suggest a growing problem about the *dependency* of a growing ageing population upon an absolutely, or relatively, declining prime-age adult population, is that many commentators make a leap from the demographic evidence to suggest a problem of economic dependency. It is suggested that there will be too few workers or pensions contributors relative to the numbers of pensions recipients.

But if attention is turned to labour force participation the key fact is that no OECD member country has much over 80% of the population aged between 15 and 64 (the OECD preferred definition of the 'working-age population') in the labour force and that there are many countries where the percentage is around two-thirds (see Table 6.4).

The simple statistical measure of the size of the labour force presented in Table 6.4 embraces a variety of phenomena:

- low labour market participation by the young because they are still in the education system;
- low labour market participation by people engaged in caring tasks, particularly here, of course, women who are caring for children;
- low labour market participation because of premature withdrawal from the labour force, either because of ill-health or because of the unavailability of work.

The last point – which is particularly important for policy proposals – was explored in the last chapter. There it was shown that the numbers

Table 6.4: Labour force participation rates in OECD countries, 2004

Country	Labour force participation rate
Australia	73.6
Austria	70.2
Belgium	65.3
Canada	78.2
Czech Republic	70.1
Denmark	80.2
Finland	73.8
France	69.5
Germany	72.7
Greece	66.5
Hungary	60.5
Ireland	68.6
Italy	62.5
Japan	72.2
Mexico	64.7
Netherlands	76.6
New Zealand	76.6
Norway	79.1
Poland	64.2
Portugal	72.9
Slovak Republic	69.7
South Korea	66.0
Spain	69.7
Sweden	78.7
Switzerland	81.0
UK	76.2
US	75.4

Note: The data is based upon a Labour Force Survey, with the labour force participation rate being all in work or wishing to be in work expressed as a percentage of the working-age population.
Source: OECD (2005a, table B, p 240)

of people outside the labour force before the official state pension age are large and have been growing. That growth has perhaps now been checked a little but not sufficiently to make a real difference to the equation we are discussing. Linked to it is also its converse – labour market participation by people over pension age. A fall in this was also noted in the last chapter, but also some signs of its reversal. Not surprisingly, therefore, countries are examining ways to increase participation in the workforce by older people, including the possibility of raising the age points at which pension entitlement starts.

Turning now to the other groups of people outside the labour force it must be noted that there are wide variations in female labour market participation. Table 6.5 highlights some European contrasts.

Table 6.5: Some indices of female employment in the European Union

Country	Female employment rate, 2000	Female rate as a % of the male rate	% of the female workforce who work part time, 2000
Austria	60.1	78	28.3
Belgium	50.3	74	40.5
Denmark	72.0	90	43.1
Finland	65.4	92	17.0
France	56.1	80	30.8
Germany	58.8	81	37.9
Greece	40.9	58	7.8
Ireland	55.0	72	30.1
Italy	41.1	60	16.5
Netherlands	65.2	79	70.4
Portugal	61.1	79	16.3
Spain	41.9	59	16.9
Sweden	70.4	96	36.0
UK	65.1	83	44.6

Sources: European Commission (2003, 2004)

Obviously many nations could increase this. Of course, then, there are questions that go beyond the concerns of this book about the desirability of such a development. The point here is that female labour force participation has been increasing steadily. Significantly, in its efforts to estimate the impact of changed labour market participation, the Pensions Commission looked at the implications of a shift in the UK level up to one comparable with Sweden (Table 6.5 shows female labour market participation there to be little different from the male rate, albeit with a significant part-time element that will be largely absent in the case of males). Of course, this may not be a valid comparison, but it is useful as an estimate of the scope for a participation increase.

As far as the labour market participation of the young is concerned, the trend in many countries has been to increase the length of periods in education; it may be questioned whether reversing this is desirable, but the point for the argument here is that in the face of a need for more workers it would be feasible to reverse it. Simplistic statements about demographic change and greater longevity focus upon the last years of life and give little attention to the extent to which the average age at which people enter the workforce is rising. In the context of the developing arguments about retirement ages it does not seem inappropriate to raise questions about the age working life starts and suggest that as much attention might be given to the length of time in the workforce as to the age at which it is left.

All of the considerations in this section may be taken into account in two different ways. The first and most obvious way is to look at the implications of changes that are occurring at the moment, and changes that may be encouraged, that increase the size of the workforce relative to the retired population. Here issues about both 'carrots' – incentives to increase participation and reduce discrimination against older workers – and 'sticks' – measures to force delays in retirement and to coerce younger people into the workforce – are on policy agendas. Inasmuch as these measures can be adopted it is, then, appropriate to amend the crude 'dependency' figures. That involves both adjusting the data to take into account actual labour force participation, and refining predictions of future developments taking into account measures that might be adopted. The Pensions Commission engages in a sophisticated way in exercises of this kind, coming to the conclusion that this can make a difference but would not entirely dispose of the concerns about an unfavourable dependency ratio. Crucial here are changes affecting both of the issues explored in the last chapter: pension age and retirement age.

But the argument so far only challenges the 'demographic time bomb' thesis in terms of evidence that if more labour force participation is needed there is a variety of places where extra workers may be found, despite the basic demographic evidence. There is a need to go beyond this to ask whether there will be this demand for more labour market participation.

Is the dependent–non-dependent relationship within a nation determined by demography?

The last section has shown that the group of people who may be able to change their status from economically inactive is substantial, and migration may also have an important impact. These facts offer a challenge to predictions about an exceptionally unfavourable ratio of dependent to non-dependent people based upon a crude demographic analysis. But that has the wider implication that these reserves of potential workers may exist as much because of lack of demand for labour as because of people's reluctance to participate in the labour force. Note in particular the evidence on social status differences in early retirement, with large numbers of workers clearly driven out of the labour force because of the lack of work.

It is odd how at the same time as the 'demographic time bomb' thesis was being developed there were other futurologists making predictions about the difficulties future economic systems would have in generating jobs. If they are right then the issues about support for 'dependants' has nothing to do with the age distribution of the population. There were massive changes in the world of work during the second half of the 20th century. These changes are likely to continue; that alone makes predicting employment patterns in 2050 difficult. It is perhaps a useful thought experiment for those of you who remember your society 40-50 years back to ask yourself if you could reasonably have predicted where it is now. I have been surprised to discover South Korean data predicting the fiscal state of their pension scheme 60 years ahead. I wonder what prediction would have been made about the current social and economic situation in Korea 60 years back in 1945!

There are many changes occurring in the world that make it very likely that employment patterns will be very different in 2050: the dramatic changes in economic activity in countries like China, the coming depletion of fossil fuel stocks, climate change and so on. Can we predict their impact? Surely we cannot. But we do not need to be able to do so to be able to say that there are very good reasons for expecting that 'dependency' will be primarily determined by the availability of work, not the age or health status or gender of the workforce.

It is recognised here that what is being challenged is a perspective held by many contemporary economists that the demand for labour can be significantly influenced by its supply. Employment trend data do not offer very strong support to that view. Middleton (2000, p 55) shows that despite adult population growth since the Second World War 'there has been no employment growth in the British economy for nearly forty years'. In any case the argument that supply can have an effect rests principally upon the use of measures that force down the cost of labour by reducing social benefit support. Obviously measures that make people wait longer for pensions will have some effects like this. But it is a massive leap from this to a perspective that assumes that coercion of people into employment will counteract all the other factors that are tending to reduce demand for labour. This argument is, of course, engaging here with some classical economic assumptions that are hard to challenge from outside. Furthermore, underlying the most optimistic version of the theory that supply will create demand is an assumption that labour productivity will increase, and that nations like the UK will be able to compete with the rest of the world in terms of 'value-added' labour. Such a view has to be underpinned by assumptions about the feasibility of continuous economic growth. This gets us into even deeper issues about economic theory. What is being offered here is not a specific prediction about the future availability of work. This observation merely raises a question that has been disregarded in discussions of the alleged problem of dependency in the future: can we be so confident that levels of labour demand will be irrelevant for the future balance between those participating in the labour force and those 'dependent' on it?

If, however, this alternative assumption provides a basis for objecting to simplistic forms of the 'demographic time bomb' argument, it also suggests implications for pension policies. If (and that 'if' should be stressed, since what is being offered is not an alternative futurology, just a suggestion that there is a need to consider alternatives to the currently conventional one) in fact there is a severe shortage of employment in the future, all approaches to protection of the retired (public and private) that rest upon contributory pensions arrangements over an extensive period of time will yield inadequate incomes for many. The problems about this approach would be, then, further increased by the far from improbable assumption, since it is already an aspect of the contemporary situation, that the impact of that shortage of employment would be likely to be differential (from place to place, occupation to occupation, class to class, gender to gender, ethnic group to ethnic group).

Of course, inasmuch as there is a possible future scenario in which there is *both* dependency as a consequence of ageing *and* dependency as a consequence of lack of work for the young, the 'crisis' scenario still needs attention. The second phenomenon would further reduce the size of the active population who are in one way or another contributing to the incomes of the inactive. It is that kind of concern that the Pensions Commission addressed when it added to the figure from which Table 6.5 above is drawn data that showed that while in 1950 the life expectancy at the time of exit from the workforce was 10.8 years for men and 16.2 years for women, by 2005 the corresponding figures were 20.4 years for men and 25.1 years for women (Pensions Commission, 2005, p 97). But the point here is that this dependency scenario may have nothing to do with the age structure of the population. Looking at this, then, from the point of views of the 'dependants' it may in any case be preferable to live in a society that regards this dependency as a consequence of age rather than as a consequence of failure to find work (a phenomenon for which there seems in our societies to be a strong propensity to blame the victim).

However, those last remarks pose even wider questions about the need to address future assumptions about 'economic' dependency as opposed to simplistic ones about demographic dependency. As far as pension policy is concerned it is difficult to go beyond that contrast to take an even wider view of the way we talk about dependency. However, if only to raise a concern about the whole tone of the dependency debate, there is a case for going a little further on the problems about a thesis that classifies the population into two groups, one dependent upon the other.

Challenging the view that those who do not participate in the labour market are 'dependent'

Simplistic statements of the 'demographic time bomb' thesis rest upon a combination of predictions about pensions, together with predictions about care needs, with a strong emphasis upon the demands these two are expected to place upon the young. But there are three problems with this perspective:

- It disregards other monetary contributions (in the widest sense including the transfer of assets), other than through employment, made by the old.
- It gives no consideration to contributions to society that are not monetised.
- It tends to exaggerate the overall dependency of the old.

As far as money is concerned the flow of resources is not simply from the young to the old. Mullan (2005) points out that pensioners may also be taxpayers, noting that a fifth of pensioners pay more in tax than they receive (taking into account both benefits and the cost of health and social care). A recent Swedish study (Fritzell and Lennartson, 2005) shows that pensioners are a major source of gifts to the young. These contributions are, of course, largely possible because of pensions (both public and private). In that sense there is a certain circularity to the argument, yet any adequate accounting of alleged future burdens needs to take into account the extent to which individuals 'give back' what they have been 'given'.

In this context it is interesting to note the extent to which the Pensions Commission views a pension entitlement as an asset (although more particularly when it is a funded private pension rather than a publicly promised PAYG one, it must be acknowledged). This leads the Commission to give very serious attention to other issues about assets, and particularly the extent of those about owner-occupied housing. It concludes, in respect of the UK, that recent growth in the value of residential housing relative to national wealth and the percentage of the housing stock that is owned by householders means that:

> Many individuals have therefore been accumulating assets through house purchase. And an increasing number are also inheriting housing assets, enabling them to support consumption in retirement through the sale of one house without losing the benefit of rent-free living in retirement. (Pensions Commission, 2005, p 86)

Not surprisingly, however, the Commission concludes that housing wealth has implications for 'appropriate pension design' but is not 'in itself a sufficient solution to problems of pension adequacy' (Pensions Commission, 2005, p 76). The point, however, for the discussion here is that dependency equations of the kind that we have been discussing, which disregard the ownership and transfer of housing assets, once again exaggerate the size of the so-called problem.

Moving on to non-monetary contributions, there is a limitation to conventional 'economistic' thinking that counts only monetised transactions. Gross Domestic Product (GDP), the conventionally used index of the prosperity of a nation, is defined as the total value of goods and in-services produced within that nation in the course of a defined period (usually a year). It does not count non-monetary productive activity and transactions. It therefore undercounts economic activity in countries where there is high use of the informal economy and of productive activity within the family. It has been ironically pointed out that if, within a household, one member starts to formally employ another to do domestic work the national GDP goes up! These activities may be outside the household too. As I write these words, my wife, a volunteer at the local hospital, is on a training course about the contribution she and others may make to the feeding of people in hospital.

Any consideration of the payment of pensions as an exchange between the generations (some discussions use an unfortunate stronger expression about the 'burden' of pensions) needs also to take into account the wide range of unremunerated roles pensioners play as carers (of the young as well as of other older people, as a number of studies of grandparent care testify) and as contributors to a wide range of voluntary activities.

Finally, another part of the 'demographic time bomb thesis' addresses itself to dependency in another sense, the issues about the health and social care needs of older people. A full discussion of the corresponding simplicity of this part of the argument would not be appropriate here (Gee and Gutman, 2000, provide a good discussion of this using Canadian data, indicating how again here the 'burden' perspective is often exaggerated). However, it is appropriate to note that the subject of the care of older people cannot be entirely separated from questions about pension adequacy. The lower the incomes of the old the less able they are to meet care costs when they arise. This has consequences for others, for their families and, of course, for public services. The use of means-tests to regulate care provision means that inadequate pensions lead to more demands on public funds.

There are different ways in which care tasks may be undertaken, which have different implications for the roles of family, market and state and accordingly very different implications for the way we count the costs of these activities. Where these tasks are absorbed within the family their costs do not feature in public accounts. They make use of people who might be active labour market participants and are instead engaged in unremunerated 'employment', and largely uncounted and unrecognised economic 'transfers' occur within families. If they are the subject of market transactions in which care is purchased, employment is generated and conventional accounting systems recognise them as being part of the economy. If they are undertaken by the state, employment is created but the general tendency of accounting systems is to see this as a cost to the private economy. There are alternative questions to be addressed about ways in which changing demographic balances will be approached in different societies. If the state is prepared to take on a large role as the provider and subsidiser of care (this in effect has been a feature of the Scandinavian model of welfare provision) then as care needs increase so too will employment increase. If this is a matter to be left to the market then the key issue for the creation of employment may be about putting those in need of care services in the best position to be able to purchase them – ironically a case for the very policy of pension enhancement that is seen as most threatened by demographic change. There is a paradox here in the context of concerns about the relationship between the so-called 'dependent' older people and the employed population, inasmuch as since the former are purchasers of services they are generators of employment! But if the issue is seen as one to be left to families then surely data on labour market participation (and also market consumption data) will become a less and less adequate measure of the amount of actual *work* being done.

My argument does not dispose of the so-called 'dependency' problem but instead asserts that (a) it will be lack of labour demand rather than demography that will be crucial and (b) it is a problem very much cast in simple economic terms, which disregard other exchanges within society.

Conclusions

This chapter started with some examination of the statistical evidence about demographic change. It went on to argue that simply estimating numbers of those of various ages likely to be alive at specific dates in the future and moving from such figures to suggestions about imbalances between the so-called dependent populations and those upon whom they will depend fails to give attention to three crucial considerations:

• There may be substantial changes in labour force participation not only on the part of older people but also on the part of younger people.
• Labour force participation is in any case likely to be heavily influenced by the demand for labour, which is difficult to predict given the continual changes in the ways in which economic activity is organised.
• Any observations on 'dependencies' between generations need to take into account much more than who does or does not work, or who does and does not pay taxes. In doing so they also need to look at exchanges of financial resources within families, and at capacities to pay for care, heavily influenced by pension arrangements.

The issue could be left here. But inasmuch as expositions of the 'demographic time bomb' thesis, which has been challenged here, go on to solutions that are also questionable – stressing the need for funding and/or a reduction of the burden on the public sector – these also need to be examined. This is done in the next chapter.

7

Facing the future:
the funding obsession

Introduction

In the last chapter it was argued that the extent to which there is an impending crisis for pension schemes has been exaggerated. In this chapter, the focus will be instead upon some of the proposals that are being advanced to deal with the alleged crisis. To discuss these may seem to show a lack of confidence in the arguments advanced in the last chapter. However, given that the crisis view is so widely accepted it is surely appropriate to go on to look at the ways it is suggested it should be addressed. They are on the agenda in any case.

In the final chapter of this book the case for a measured package of responses to fears about the future will be advanced; here the emphasis is upon one particular group of approaches. These are encapsulated in a quotation from Estelle James, lead author of the World Bank report described in Chapter Four. She argues: 'Some degree of pre-funding is desirable in an old age security system. This helps to insulate the system from demographic shock' (James, 2001, p 63). That is quite a measured version of a view that has been reproduced in many journalistic essays on the future of pensions as an argument that only by way of more saving and investing (usually seen as investing in the private sector) can we protect ourselves against the demographic time bomb. These views, then, find echoes in government proposals for pension system change all over the world in which funding is on the agenda (see, for example, the discussion of Sweden in Chapter Four). In the case of the UK, where there is already a substantial funded private pensions sector, the corresponding focus is upon ways in which the government can increase the contribution that sector makes to overall pension provision.

The central place in most conventional analyses of this issue is taken by concerns about the way in which the burden upon government will increase. The OECD, the European Union and individual governments have all published predictions about how this burden will rise. Table 7.1 sets out one such prediction, a European Union one reproduced by the Pensions Commission. Obviously there are various ways of predicting a future burden, all of which have elements of inaccuracy, depending as they do upon efforts not merely to make the right demographic assumptions but also upon assumptions about the economic factors that will influence contributions and benefits. The latter are important given the tendency

Table 7.1: Predictions of future public pension expenditure as a % of GDP in the European Union, made in 2001

	2000 (rough actual)	2010	2030	2050	2050 figure as % of 2000
Austria	14.5	14.9	18.1	17.0	117
Belgium	10.0	9.9	13.3	13.3	133
Denmark	10.5	12.5	14.5	13.3	127
Finland	11.3	11.6	14.9	15.9	141
France	12.1	13.1	16.0	Missing	132+
Germany	11.8	11.2	15.5	16.9	143
Greece	12.6	12.6	19.6	24.8	197
Italy	13.8	13.9	15.7	14.1	102
Luxembourg	7.4	7.5	9.2	9.3	126
Netherlands	7.9	9.1	13.1	13.6	172
Portugal	9.4	11.8	13.6	13.2	140
Spain	9.4	8.9	12.6	17.3	184
Sweden	9.0	9.6	11.4	10.7	119
UK	5.5	5.1	5.2	4.4	80

Source: EU Economic Policy Committee, 2001, reported in Pensions Commission (2004)

for expenditure predictions to be expressed as percentages of GDP, since future GDP is particularly hard to predict. Naturally predictions also have to use current pension scheme rules in order to predict expenditure in the future, even though these are changing all the while. They can hardly be criticised for this since one of their objectives is to help governments consider the case for making changes.

Clearly the common element in relation to these estimates is the demographic trend, but with the proportion of older people rising at different rates in different countries and predicted to peak at different times; hence, the suggestion that the growth will flatten or even stop between 2030 and 2050. However, do not forget that demographic predictions fall in accuracy the further you try to look ahead.

But what, of course, a comparative chart particularly does is focus attention upon national differences and thus upon the impact of public policy differences. In this case there are obviously two important issues here: public pension scheme generosity, and the extent of dependence upon public as opposed to private pension arrangements. Where the figures are particularly high it is generally the case that it is the presence of universal public schemes with earnings-related coverage that extends well up the income distribution that are a source of high costs to the government now and will be a big influence on cost growth.

What is striking here is the way in which the UK stands out as a country where there will be no cost growth. While it is important to bear in mind the comments above about variability of predictions, since other predictions do show some growth, there is general agreement that the UK has at the moment a system that offers no, or very little, threat to efforts to control public expenditure growth. This is primarily because of the very low levels of state provision, not evidence of some hidden demographic difference. In terms of coverage at the bottom of the income distribution it has little catching up to do; at the same time it offers little in the way of income replacement for higher income earners. What is particularly significant is obviously the presence of a strong private pension system. The basic evidence on this in relation to current expenditure was reported in Chapter Four (Table 4.2).

Much has been made in the UK press about the contrast between the UK and Germany in this respect. The high public liabilities within the German scheme (but, of course, also in other public social insurance schemes) have been argued to be a potential source of problems for the European Union in the future, an argument that delights in contrasting what is presented as a UK virtue and a German vice. The analysis of the credibility of this argument poses difficult questions both about economics and about how the European Union is run. The general issue, however, brings us to the crucial question: does the absence of a potential public expenditure problem also imply an absence of an overall problem in the face of demographic change?

At one level the answer to that question is obviously 'yes'. The absence of an increased public sector burden implies the absence of a need to increase taxation or social insurance contributions to maintain existing pension commitments. Here we could then get into deeper philosophical discussion about whether increased taxation matters, but let us leave it that there is a very widely expressed view that it does. That position, however, may be challenged if it is the case that there is a cost to be paid for the absence of additional taxation. One such cost is the cost in terms of inferior pensions. The cost to be discussed here involves a question about the extent to which pensions not paid for out of the public purse will impose costs upon future generations of workers.

This chapter will advance the view that the case for funding is widely exaggerated (the expression 'funding' will be used here without a prefix, following the definition of this phenomenon used by the Pensions Commission, and cited in Chapter Four, in which the 'pre-' is implicit). The presentation will start from a discussion of what funding really implies for the future. It will present some basic macro-economics that can be found in many official publications these days (including reports from the OECD and the UK Pensions

Commission) but which continue to be ignored in many popular presentations of the issues.

It will then go on to explore arguments for and against funding. In doing so it will distinguish between different kinds of funding. It will recognise that much of the argument for funding is presented – as noted above – as involving investment in the private sector (probably under the control of that sector), and will argue that this need not be the case. It will also argue that much of the case for funding is made in terms of specific individual accounts and suggest that this is also not an essential feature of funding.

It will end with some comments on why funding lies at the very core of the reform agenda, and argue that (while realism is necessary about the strength of an already existing set of economic and political actors) such views need not drive the overall reform agenda.

Funding and the future

The desirability of funding has become almost an unchallengeable principle in debates about contemporary pension policy. It is seen as a virtuous approach to the future in its own right, just as it is often seen as virtuous for individuals to save. But what applies to individuals does not necessarily apply to societies. When we save in any scheme, public or private, we are simply trading a contribution to contemporary expenditure against a promise to pay us something in the future. Money is not stored in vaults against the day we want it back. It is worth bearing in mind that the quaint statement on the back of British bank notes that the Bank of England 'promises to pay the bearer' may be just a survival from the days of gold but it is also a reminder that money only has value in respect of the goods it will eventually purchase.

Pension contributions are savings. When we save we invest. Sometimes we do this directly but very often indirectly, we give our money to an organisation for safe keeping and it does the investing.

The security of that money, and above all its growth to protect us from the effects of inflation, depends upon that investment.

What then happens when we want our money back? If the investment is in property the situation is that there may need to be a sale of that property to facilitate the shift back into liquid funds. A satisfactory sale – meaning a payment of the value of the original investment plus growth – depends upon the willingness of buyers to pay the appropriate price. This can be seen most vividly with a rather odd kind of asset – an antique. Viewers of programmes about antiques may observe that people have enjoyed healthy growth in the values of their antiques. But this growth will only be sustained if there is a steady flow of new potential purchasers into the antiques market.

However, pension fund investors do not confine investments to property. Much investment is in economic enterprises of some kind. Thus, it supports the productivity of others. In this case when we want our money back, while the same arguments about the need for alternative investors apply, the issues are also about the extent to which our demands for money have an impact upon the activities of those who have used it. We are engaged in taking out some of the profits of enterprise, and this may be at the expense of wages. Again, then, the key issue for future predictions is about the incoming contributions from new investors to replace the outgoing payments to pensioners. In this case the hope is that in the meantime economic growth may soften the negative impact of any imbalance. This point is spelt out because of one of the issues about demographic change: if the future prospect is of an excess of people wanting to liquidise assets because of a need for income flows in old age, what appears to be a simple way of protecting assets may prove deficient.

When we make pension contributions we are paying a very long way in advance for things we will need in the future. An examination of 20th-century history reveals various situations – wars, economic crises, runaway inflation – when that would have been a rash thing to do. It will not be argued here that it is necessarily rash to invest. Rather, what needs to be emphasised here is that the very strongly made case for investment is based on an alternatively very complacent view that the risks are minimal.

The intention here is to underline the extent to which funding arrangements depend upon secure expectations of the future. In the doomsday scenario from the private sector side of the argument the future problem is seen to be that governments will be unable to meet their obligations, a perspective that only makes sense in the context of a related belief that there are – these days – severe limits upon government capacities to increase taxation. At the same time the advocates of private solutions disregard the potential economic problems – with similar costs very like increased taxation for workers – that will arise if the payment obligations of private schemes rise sharply.

The Pensions Commission (2005, p 164) endorses this logic in a curious way, saying:

> All pension schemes, PAYG or funded, entail a transfer of resources from future workers to future pensioners. In a PAYG scheme workers pay taxes to provide pensions. In a funded scheme future workers buy accumulated assets from retirees.

That last point will seem a little obscure; accumulated investments are, of course, assets, but, as suggested above, their worth depends upon either the productivity of the future generations or their readiness to replace the withdrawn savings of pensioners with new investments of their own. Barr (2002, p 4) puts the point more succinctly:'individuals must exchange current production for a claim on future production' hence 'both funded and pay-as-you-go plans are claims on future output, and they are of no use to retirees if the country is not producing enough goods and services to meet those claims'.

What, then, is the case for funding?

The Pensions Commission advances four arguments for funding:

(1) 'People may be more willing to accept ... savings into an account which is legally theirs, and the value of which is defined in clear capital terms, than to accept taxation to support a PAYG system' (Pensions Commission, 2005, p 164).

(2) The existence of funds imposes a measure of discipline on governments otherwise inclined to spend PAYG receipts now and leave others to worry about future obligations.

(3) Individual funding increases private choice for savers.

(4) Explicit funding, if invested in part overseas, can enable a society in aggregate to build up pension claims on other countries, providing some escape from the otherwise unavoidable challenge of a rising dependency ratio' (Pensions Commission, 2005, p 166).

Those arguments all look at the issue of funding from the point of view of securing satisfactory pension systems. To these may be added:

(5) Other arguments that address the case for funding as desirable for the growth of the economy. These take us into some complex economic issues beyond the scope of this book. Some limited observations will be made on these arguments (readers should refer to chapters 7 and 8 of Barr, 2001, and to Beattie and McGillivray, 1995, for fuller critiques).

In relation to all these points, questions about variations in the forms funding takes will require attention.

(1) Acceptability to savers

Any discussion of acceptability to savers brings us up against the ideological divide outlined in Chapter One, and revisited in many places in this book. Having regard to preferences for saving into specific accounts as opposed to taxation must involve seeing pensions as saved or withheld individual remuneration. Any pension arrangements built around strict adherence to this point will carry forward the inequalities within working life into retirement. So, as suggested in Chapter One, the policy question is about how much strict regard for the interests of savers will be modified in practice. The interesting issue about funding is whether – as opposed to the idea of allowing the operation of two quite separate pension tiers (as explored in Chapter Four) – forms of funding can be operated in which there is some pooling between contributors as opposed to the strict maintenance of separate accounts, which will still be acceptable to savers. If this is achievable the result will be – regardless of what is or is not done to invest funds – not wildly different from that embodied in the German social insurance scheme (and the Swedish one before its recent reforms).

(2) Discipline on governments

There is a distinction that needs to be made in respect of this argument between having a system in which our contributions are properly registered, and the pension promises that follow from them are adhered to, and actual funding involving the investing of money. The issue here is one about how much we trust government to honour promises (many years after they were made, by perhaps a government of a very different ideological colour). I put this to a group of students once in the form of the question: which are you more inclined to trust, the government or capitalism? A wit at the back of the class replied 'neither'. He had a point, but then his problem would be how to protect resources when ultimately some combination of economic development and governmental actions would determine their long-run value.

But coming back to the issue of discipline on governments, there is a quite widely favoured view that the best way to control funding is through an organisation independent of government (see, for example, the views of Frank Field, 2006, and the Pensions Reform Group). A number of European governments have set up arrangements that combine laws to protect funds from interference with independent managerial arrangements. In many respect this is no more than carrying forward the approach to the protection of social insurance, involving representatives of the 'social partners' as in Germany and France, into a new world in which funding is also used. Any consideration of the merits of this has probably to be combined with examination of the issues about pooling raised in connection with point (1).

(3) Choice for savers

The Pensions Commission's third point about choice can only really be seen as a case for individual accounts invested in the private sector, through intermediary organisations likely to be similarly private in character. The compromise alternatives outlined in relation to the last two points cannot really apply here (except inasmuch as individuals may be invited to make choices to forego individual gains for the collective good). There are some issues here about the extent to which informed choices can be made in the pension funds 'jungle', to which we return in the last chapter.

(4) Spreading national risks

The Pensions Commission goes on to note the particular attraction of the funding option for small countries (noting the Swedish use of the investment of 'buffer funds' overseas). The use of this argument for funding is interesting in running against an alternative argument used by the World Bank in favour of funding: that it contributes to current investment and thus the enhancement of national economic growth, something of particular value in developing economies where investments are low and there are few alternative sources of them. In practice the development of the global market for investments surely suggests that in neither case can it be guaranteed that investments remain where they start off, but that is a more cogent argument against the World Bank's point than it is against the basic argument for spreading risks. Since this argument is being used by the Pensions Commission in favour of funding, it must, however, be seen as in some respects a variant of its second argument. A case for funding abroad (as opposed to the operation of a PAYG scheme) implies not simply a lack of confidence in the national economy but also a lack of confidence in the national government.

(5) Strengthening the economy

As noted above, there have been many quite technical economic arguments for and against pension funding for the good of the economy. The case in favour is made in terms of the contributions that flows of pension savings make to investments and thereby to economic growth. It is hard to find fault in principle that if our economy is strengthened then it will find it easier to meet our needs in future. Moreover, echoing the discussion in the last section, if our long-run welfare depends upon global growth the global use of pension funds is to be welcomed.

It is beyond the concerns of this book to go into the more detailed aspects of this argument, about how the money is actually used and about whether there is a straightforward flow of pension funds into economy-strengthening investments. But what should be noted are some statistics that suggest that it does not seem to be self-evident that extensive funded pension systems are crucial for national investment. These were presented in Table 4.2 in Chapter Four. The question they raise is: if funding is so vital for the economy, how can it be the case that pension fund investments remain very low in quite a number of countries (Germany, Japan and so on)? If the argument is that state-run PAYG pension systems are bad for economies and private funded ones are good, then why are the countries where the former are dominant not laggards in respect of economic growth. Surely the argument for pension funds as necessary saving needs to be modified by the examination of the other ways in which some nations save and invest. Of course, the accumulation of pension funds may be a good way of getting investable money into the market, but it is certainly not the only way.

It would seem to be the case that an argument that may apply in the societies where pension funds are key elements in the financial markets – and, of course, in particular the UK and the US – has been expressed as a universally applicable truth. But then even in those societies it may be questioned whether it is essential that this development continues, with such funds rising ever upwards. The fact that such funds exist means that there is, of course, an interest group – those who make their incomes investing funds – who may have a significant impact on public policy. One US Nobel prize-winning economist, Joseph Stiglitz (2005), has warned against this interest group, seeing them as obviously only too eager 'to grab a piece' of the growing 'transaction' costs involved in the investment of pension funds.

Yet, it may be that the heyday of ever-growing pension funds has passed. The more uncertain returns on the stock markets have reduced the attractiveness of individual funded pensions. The growing transaction costs are seen as increasingly problematical. Then, what governments that combine pro-market sentiments with a wish to satisfy demands for better pensions for middle- and lower-income people want is a lowering of those costs. There does seem the possibility that the private pension providers will be reluctant to extend their activities in this way. This is an issue that is crucial for the UK pension reforms to be discussed in the next chapter.

We are back here, then, to the need to differentiate the arguments about funding from those about private funding. Blackburn (2002) has advanced an argument for a 'socialist' road towards state investment of pension funds, as opposed to the alternative shift, encouraged by the World Bank, of encouraging increased privatisation of pension systems. The case for such an approach was widely advocated in the Swedish Social Democratic Party. In the end it opted for a compromise in respect of pensions, not only in confining the funded element to a small share in the total pension scheme but also by opting for private investing in the context of a state-controlled structure. Again that point will not be explored further. This is a book about pensions, written from a perspective of concern about pension policy from a social policy rather than economic perspective, not a tract on how to manage or control capitalism.

Funding and the future economy

It was argued earlier that demographic change will impose similar strains whether there is funding or not. Self-evidently, without funding it is public expenditure that will have to take the strain, with knock-on effects for taxation and personal consumption. It is appropriate to say a little more here about the corresponding issues for states where there has been substantial funding. It has been suggested that there may be substantial disinvestment if there is an imbalance between the withdrawal of pension funds and new investment. This may then have adverse consequences for future workers. These may take a variety of forms: actual decreases in the returns from work as funds reclaim what are in effect 'profits', damage to enterprise as a result of inadequate investment flows and perhaps consequent unemployment or a need for current workers to pay more into depleted pension funds in order to protect their own pensions. There is also a consequence for potential pensioners within defined contribution schemes: that on sale (to realise income) their investments realise less than expected, since this is the likely effect in a market in which there are more sellers than buyers. If the expected imbalance between pension recipients and investors were a temporary one the points here would have less force but this may not be the case. While the demographic projections do indicate a point at which the alleged adverse trends end, they do not suggest a dramatic reversal. That could only come about with a significant upward shift in the birth rate, currently an unlikely scenario and obviously another unknown for this discussion.

Some advantages flowing from investment outside a country have been noted above. Those advantages may extend to help to deal with the fact that a country may well experience demographic change and a downturn in the economy at the same time. However, the demographic shift is a worldwide phenomenon with the strongest combinations of both increased longevity and falling birth rates occurring in some of the countries where recent economic change has been dramatic. Note, for example, how one of the largest and most strongly growing economies today – China – is also a country where previous efforts to reduce the birth rate have been the most purposeful, imposing a one child per family restriction upon most urban Chinese. That country will in due course experience an extraordinarily strong shift in its demographically defined dependency ratios.

It is appropriate to digress here to look at a related point about another private form of protection, aside from investments in private pension schemes – protection for individuals and families that may be secured through investment in owner-occupied housing (perhaps a form of investment that the student quoted above as trusting neither capitalism nor the government had in mind). The Pensions Commission gave quite a lot of attention to this issue, recognising that the big growth in owner-occupation in the UK through the second half of the 20th century has added to factors that will mitigate the effects of the demographic shift. How much they do so is hard to calculate. We are talking here of a combination of benefits accruing as such assets pass from generation to generation, given that these days many people lose their last surviving parent around the time they retire, and given ways in which such assets may be accessed in advance through trading down to cheaper houses and through remortgaging arrangements. This topic is complicated by the ways in which assets are taken into account in social care means-tests, so some may use up housing assets paying for care at the end of life. However, the key point is that the snag about investment withdrawal also applies in this case: an excess of sellers over buyers may also reduce house prices. It may seem a bit strange to identify this as a problem at a time when house price inflation in the UK has been considerable (both from a long-run and a short-run perspective) and there is clear evidence of a shortage of homes for all who want them. But this point is being made in a context of a long-run shift in the size of the prime-age population relative to the old, and this shift must to some extent choke off demand for new housing. Unfortunately also much housing need arises at the bottom end of the market where house purchase is difficult and in a situation in which much of the cheapest owner-occupied housing is decreasing in value (against the general trend) because it is deteriorating or is in areas where there is no employment. This reminds us that despite the widespread owner-occupation in the UK, much of the housing that promises to provide a substantial capital gain is possessed by those whose pension protection is generally good.

Overall, the investment strategies that commend themselves to cautious pension fund managers involve a mixture of investments. These may reduce the dangers from the biggest changes, but they do so at the price – which applies to any hedging of bets – that returns will be lower. It is significant that one of the particular strategies that has been widely favoured to protect pension funds in the UK has been to put a percentage of the investment into government funds. The irony about this is that inasmuch as this is the case the private funds may be contributing to the long-run problem of increased pressure on public expenditure since disinvestment in this field reduces the funds available to the government.

PAYG as an alternative

The aim in the discussion so far in this chapter has been to suggest that while much attention is being given to the impact of demographic changes for public expenditure, with many writers going from that to make the point that private pension schemes should be seen as a preferred option, the impact of this upon private pensions may well also be quite considerable. How much this is the case is something that economists seem somehow reluctant to assess. Reality here may be brought home to societies like the UK's a long while in the future. However, there are considerations about the protection of individuals on which it is easier to address the pros and cons of public and private arrangements. These were to a considerable extent the concerns of Chapter Four, in which some attention was given to the large groups who are unlikely to be able to be investors in private pensions. That in itself would be an argument for a dual system – public pensions for the less well off, private ones for the better off. We return to this issue in the conclusions to this book (Chapter Eight).

But this chapter has focused upon the issues about funding in a way that implicitly compares this approach to PAYG (in terms of impact on individuals, economies and societies). Crucial for the defence of PAYG (or indeed for highly modified forms of funding that operate in a collective way rather than in terms of very specific individual funds) is the extent to which such schemes can be more inclusive. They can then avoid, or at least reduce the extent of, the problem that a division tends to emerge between funded schemes for the better off and minimum pensions for the rest. The case for this is embodied in a classic argument in favour of universalism in social policy, that where there are shared interests in shared policy provisions on the part of the well off as well as poorer people the provisions for the latter are better (Korpi and Palme, 1998).

A more pragmatic case is made for widespread public provision of protection through social insurance using PAYG by Myles (2002), who argues that the best approach to the issue of a fair deal between the generations is – assuming present relativities between the income flow to the old and the pension contributions (both public and private) being made by the workforce – a formula that changes both pensions and contributions over time to maintain those relativities. Hence, if we reach a time when the size of the dependent generation rises rapidly then the cost of that can be proportionately shared between those who pay and those who receive benefits. It is an equation of this kind that the German government has been trying to achieve in its social insurance reforms. Myles goes on to argue that this solution will be the easiest for governments to adopt, given the pressures upon them to both minimise tax increases and minimise pension cuts.

But then an important aspect of Myles' argument for the alternatives being considered here is that, where pension schemes are substantially privatised, while the direct political problems for governments may be less there may be very acute problems of equity as market forces affect different groups differently. He argues that 'in a totally privatised system based on advance funding and other personal assets' problems of cost allocation between the generations would be solved 'by producing lucky and less lucky generations'. Hence:

> Some cohorts and individuals would benefit from favourable wage histories and returns to their capital and so be in a position to retire early. Other cohorts and individuals would be less fortunate and be required to work longer to avoid an impoverished retirement. (Myles, 2002, p 139)

However, it has to be recognised here that, while it is to be hoped that within the increasingly money market-dominated politics of the European Union the German approach to pension provision will not come under threat, the UK is on a pathway on which a turn back to that model is no longer likely. Probably from Beveridge onwards it was inevitable that policy making on contributory pensions would involve a compromise between the public and private sectors; certainly the last chance to go down the German road was lost in the 1960s.

Conclusions

The original idea was to subtitle this chapter 'the funding illusion'; this was rejected in favour of 'obsession'. The element of 'illusion' is that funding explicitly secures pension contributions against social and economic changes. But there are things to be said for funding. A great deal, then, depends upon how funding systems are operated. There is a case to be made for the collective investment of pensions contributions, making future expectations as clear as possible while at the same time reducing disadvantages and risks for those only able to make low contributions. Yet much of the literature advocating funding operates with a very individualist model. This leads to a conclusion that the combination of concerns about future economic and social uncertainty with an aspiration to operate pension systems in a progressive way that is not socially divisive tends to support the continued case for the PAYG approach as embodied in the sophisticated social insurance systems of several Continental European countries. That does not, however, offer an easy way out of the UK dilemma, to which we return in the final chapter.

On the other hand, it is definitely an illusion to see funding as offering a universal panacea for pension problems that may arise from demographic change.

8

Pension reform

Introduction

This chapter brings this book to a conclusion through an examination of the outstanding challenges to pension policy worldwide, an exploration of the UK government's current reform proposals and finally some personal conclusions by the author.

The stance throughout the book has been to see pension policy issues as:

- involving conflicts between views of pensions as essentially deferred earned income and as ways of ensuring adequate incomes for all in old age, with actual policies being varying compromises between these two perspectives;
- complicated by the ways in which public and private arrangements exist side by side;
- following 'pathways' established early in the history of government interventions from which politicians have difficulties in diverging given the high costs involved and the need to combine current concerns with a long-term perspective.

The examination of the history of pensions shows a steady growth in complexity in which reform proposals have to relate to elaborate existing systems and difficult problems about forecasting future effects but sit within what are very often short-term political agendas. The applicability of that generalisation will, of course, vary from place to place; some nations (for reasons linked to their political and institutional structures) seem to be better at handling these issues

(Sweden and Germany seem to offer model cases). The history of pension policy in the UK suggests that it lies at the extreme other end in this respect; there have been many twists and turns of policy and a range of incremental changes that are often poorly related to each other.

The contemporary pension debate is very influenced by predictions about the impact of demographic change. These were questioned in Chapter Six. Responses to that issue are very often cast in terms of a need to increase the funded element in pension systems. The dominance of that perspective was challenged in Chapter Seven. Pension reform is now widely seen as about the downgrading of pension promises and the cutting of the pension costs that will have to be met by governments through tax and social insurance increases. Various comparative studies casting the issues in these terms will be discussed below. In this context drastic approaches to cutting are seen as inhibited by political risk aversion (this is something effectively explored in an edited book of national case studies by Bonoli and Shinkawa, 2005).

However, cost cutting is not the only concern on the agenda. Many governments are still in situations in which they confront issues about pension scheme improvement. It is here that issues about pension adequacy for all are on the agenda. Hence, actual system changes are likely to involve combinations of efforts at cost control with efforts to improve the coverage of pension schemes. The examination later in this chapter of the UK reform agenda exemplifies this.

The worldwide debate

A review of pension reform worldwide by two OECD staff members records a wide range of changes to pension systems, describing the 'main, although not sole, motivation for reform' as 'to strengthen the financial sustainability of public pension systems' (Whiteford and Whitehouse, 2006, p 89). They emphasise the importance of cuts but indicate that 'For obvious political reasons, these changes have exploited the complexity of pensions to reduce future benefits in less-than-transparent ways' (p 89). They go on to list a wide range of types of changes:

- 'Changes in the number of years used in benefit calculations.'
- 'Changing the valorization of past earnings.'
- 'Changing the indexation of pensions in payment.'
- 'Linking pensions to higher life expectancy.'
- 'Increasing pension eligibility age.'
- 'Increasing the reward for continuing in work.'
- 'Introducing mandatory Defined Contribution plans.'

The key context for these changes is the demographic shift discussed in Chapters Five and Six. Its specific impact upon pension schemes across the nations is set out in Table 8.1 in terms of changes already occurring.

There are, then, various attempts to project that forward: Table 7.1 in Chapter Seven did this in respect of various European countries.

While there is no doubt that it is cutting that dominates the world pensions agenda there is a need to draw a distinction between the way such an agenda manifests itself where pension arrangements are already generally adequate and its implications in situations in which there are still problems about coverage. It would certainly be rash to take some of the big growth figures in Table 7.1 and conclude that the problem is that those countries are too generous. The real growth recorded in some countries in Table 7.1 – for example in Greece or Spain – may suggest costs arising from ongoing improvements to coverage.

Comparative data on coverage are much less accessible. Some evidence on adequacy was quoted in Chapter Three, but it was also suggested there that many of the issues about extent of coverage are complex, in which case comparative material cannot easily do them justice. The OECD study from which Table 3.2 in that chapter was taken engages in an exercise to compare systems in terms of 'progressivity', that is the extent to which there is redistribution towards lower earners within schemes. They suggest high levels in

Table 8.1: Public pension spending as a % of GDP in various OECD countries

	1980	2001	% increase
Australia	3.2	4.1	28
Austria	8.5	10.3	21
Belgium	6.1	8.6	41
Canada	3.1	4.8	55
Denmark	5.8	6.5	11
Finland	4.7	7.1	51
France	7.6	10.4	37
Germany	9.8	10.8	10
Greece	5.1	12.6	147
Italy	7.4	11.2	38
Japan	2.9	6.4	121
Netherlands	6.5	5.7	−12
Spain	4.6	8.1	76
Sweden	6.6	6.8	3
Switzerland	5.6	11.6	107
UK	5.1	7.7	20
US	5.1	5.2	2

Source: Whiteford and Whitehouse (2006), using OECD material from the Social Expenditure database.

respect of countries with flat-rate pensions (New Zealand) or with targeted or basic pension schemes (Australia, Canada, Denmark and the UK). However, progressivity in itself may not be enough where the minimum income guaranteed is very low, or where some people are excluded from access to even that (the OECD study compares wage earners). Table 3.3 in the same chapter, looking at pensioner poverty, suggests at least no grounds for complacency in the case of the UK (nations outside the European Union do not figure in those statistics); furthermore, as the UK pension reform debate suggests, progressivity may come at a cost in terms of the demeaning or deterrent effects of means-testing. It is not appropriate to conclude that a system that is low cost and progressive has necessarily got its pension policy right.

So the general conclusion to draw from this brief incursion into comparative material on issues relating to pension reform is that this may well take not the simple form of seeking ways to impose cuts to public costs but the more complex form of efforts to cut benefits to, or increase contributions from, some groups while at the same time making improvements for others. This is evidently the case where pension arrangements are still very embryonic but may also apply in some of the more differentiated mature systems, of which the UK is a prime example.

If the pension reform agenda is first and foremost seen as a combination of a search for ways to do more and ways to do less, it is important to recognise that its relationship to the widely expressed arguments in favour of funding, probably linked to privatisation, will not be a straightforward one. This view was explored in the last chapter. The adoption of those devices inevitably has some effects: making the achievement of ways to support those unable to be significant contributors more difficult (if not impossible), shifting costs and not necessarily cutting benefits but probably making them less predictable. There are also likely to be long delays before changes of this kind reach their full impact. On the other hand, it is equally possible that simple public PAYG schemes will be inadequate and inequitable (many are already) and that reforms linked to government parsimony will make them worse.

In any case it was argued in Chapter Seven that it is fallacious to regard either privatisation or pre-funding (or both) as essential for future pension scheme viability. Nevertheless, much of the conventional debate about pension reform involves arguments about its necessity set out either in terms of the avoidance of unsustainable burdens for the public sector or as ways to ensure a vibrant future economy. Hence, these issues arise as aspects of the reform debate in various places, as phenomena that affect the measures adopted.

In the real world of pension politics proposals tend to involve combinations of approaches. The pure private road, just leaving us to solve our future pension problems ourselves, exists only in the wilder dreams of the New Right. In the real world the contemporary exploration of ways to advance the private market model usually involves the combination of exploration of ways for the state to enhance a private investment approach with some significant public regulation and underpinning. It is particularly embodied in the World Bank's pillars model. At the other extreme, within the public model – perhaps most clearly embodied in the German scheme – there is nevertheless a reluctance to regard PAYG as a problem for future generations. Moreover, it is interesting to note how one of the traditionally strong and inclusive public schemes – that of Sweden – has come to embrace both elements of pre-funding and some privatisation.

The UK reform agenda

Chapter Two (as reinforced by the further discussion of issues of adequacy in Chapter Three) left the historical account of the UK pension system at the point where it was not working very well, given the peculiar combination of:

- state provision through a seriously eroded flat-rate basic pension reinforced by an additional contributory State Second Pension and underpinned by the means-tested pension credit; and
- private but optional provisions largely only attractive to above-average earners.

The government launched a thorough investigation of the system by the Pensions Commission in 2002, which provided a very detailed initial assessment of the situation in 2004 and a carefully documented set of recommendations in 2005. In a White Paper responding to this work the government repeated the Pensions Commission's judgement that the UK system is 'the most complex in the World' (DWP, 2006, p 13). It went on to outline some proposals for change that, while arguably they will not reduce complexity very much, aim to deal with what the government sees as the key problems about the system. At the time this book is going to press these are being translated into legislation, but with a leisurely timetable to accommodate a quite complex implementation process.

There are differences between the Pensions Commission's proposals for reform and those adopted by the government. It is not particularly illuminating for a book of this kind to go into a full comparison of the two approaches. So attention will here be primarily upon the White Paper's proposals.

Understandably the White Paper starts with a defence of the existing system and of the steps taken by the Blair governments to improve it since 1997. But it then goes on to acknowledge a case for reform in terms of:

- the implications of demographic and social change;
- evidence on the extent of undersaving for retirement;
- inequalities in the state pension system;
- complexity.

Some data rather crucial for the overall analysis are reported on levels of saving (meaning largely saving by way of private pension fund contributions) that are seen as likely to leave significant numbers with inadequate incomes in old age and to have in fact fallen since the end of the 1970s. This leads the government to a prediction about the pension credit, which it presents as its key contribution to the reduction of 'absolute poverty' (its term), that if current arrangements continued 'the proportion of pensioner households entitled to Pension Credit would increase from around 45 per cent today to around 70 per cent by 2050' (DWP, 2006, p 41, para 1.34). It goes on to the following interesting comment on its own policy:

> The potential future spread of Pension Credit could reduce
> incentives to save for some people. However, it has never
> been the Government's intention to move over the long
> term towards a system where a significant majority of

> pensioners are entitled to Pension Credit. (DWP, 2006,
> p 41, para 1.35)

The government's agenda may thus be seen as framed in terms of (a) the issue of undersaving (which its earlier stakeholder pensions initiative had failed to reverse) and (b) the fact that the main plank in its current policies to deal with pensioner poverty is the means-tested pension credit. The undersaving issue is obviously its key concern but it acknowledges the contradiction to that approach embodied in its anti-poverty policy.

The UK pensions debate may be seen as involving two opposing perspectives. One of these has as its key plank the raising of the basic state pension to a level at which it (rather than a means-tested scheme deterring saving) would be the main device to prevent pensioner poverty. The other is the advocacy of ways to secure much higher levels of pension saving by lower-income people. The Pensions Commission may, broadly speaking, be seen as adopting both. It argues for new private pension savings arrangements at lower costs and with government support and control, and for improvement in the basic state pension (traded off against an increase in the pension age). The White Paper adopted that perspective, but with the pension savings proposal as a central plank and some rather more complex changes to state pensions (also to be traded off against a pension age increase). Immediately after the publication of the Pensions Commission's second report in 2005 the Chancellor had allowed his staff to leak his concern about the cost of its proposal; the White Paper offers a complex (cost-controlled) way forward towards a better basic pension.

The pension savings system proposed is, on the face of it, relatively straightforward (although we may well find that 'the devil will reside' in the future administrative details). It is a system of personal pension savings accounts to which employees will contribute 4% of a band of earnings between £5,000 and £33,000 a year. To these employers will add an equivalent 3%. There will be an additional 1% from the government, although it is acknowledged that this is merely the equivalent of basic rate tax relief as already the minimum given to private pension contributions. This will not be a compulsory scheme but there will be what the government calls 'automatic enrolment' from which employees will have to explicitly opt out. Employers will not be able to opt out unless their employees do so. This money will then be invested and, while the White Paper indicates that there is a need for yet further exploration of the way the personal account scheme will be managed through private sector investment companies, the aim will be to keep the management costs low. There will be choices of funds, underpinned by a 'default fund' for those who do not exercise choice (a group found to be quite large in the scheme of this kind operated in Sweden). The issue of administrative costs is important, as the White Paper shows with some specific comparisons, because the high management costs that apply to many current investment schemes of this kind can seriously reduce a pension. This can have particularly serious consequences for people only able to contribute relatively small amounts, and in the private sector, as it operates at present, it is the case that management charges tend to be proportionately higher for such people.

So the key proposal aims to get more lower-income earners into the private pension system. This measure does not extend to the self-employed, is likely to offer little to low earners from part-time and casual work and will be voluntary.

The accompanying proposals for state pensions aim to increase the numbers who qualify for them and to eventually lead to a situation where means-testing is reduced. However, the route to that goal is slow and the proposals complex and with much lower costs falling upon the government than would be involved in any straightforward increasing of the basic pension entitlement. The key to understanding them depends largely on understanding the way the State Second Pension works, a topic on which the White Paper admits there is little understanding:

> Few people are aware of it at all, and even fewer of how their entitlement to it builds. Many people are building

entitlement to the State Second Pension without even being aware they are doing so. (DWP, 2006, p 116, para 3.46)

As far as the basic pension is concerned the proposal is to reduce the qualifying period so that only 30 years' contributions are needed to secure the full pension. This change is linked with improvements to the way credits of contributions operate for those caring for children and for disabled people. These measures are important to increase access to state pensions for people, particularly women, not able to participate fully enough in the labour force to qualify under present arrangements.

But such improvements will be limited in impact so long as the basic state pension remains well below the subsistence level guaranteed by the pension credit. So then what does the White Paper have to say about the uprating of this? In fact all that is offered is the start of a change back to uprating the basic pension in line with earnings from 2012 (hedging even that with the weasel clause 'subject to affordability and the fiscal position'; we will come back to that below). That means an incremental year-by-year shift upwards that pays no attention to the long period over which the basic pension has fallen in value since that uprating principle was abandoned in 1979. Moreover, since the proposal is to apply the same uprating principle to pension credit the change will do nothing to reduce the gap between the values of the two pensions.

However, that is where it becomes important to look at what is happening to, and proposed for, the State Second Pension. That pension, as was noted in Chapter Two, is an improved version of the SERPS designed to offer some protection to low earners. It works with graduated contributions and graduated benefits subject to a minimum for the latter. Individuals in private pension schemes deemed by the government to be adequate alternatives can opt out of contributing to it. The implications of the scheme for a significant proportion of its contributors is that they will eventually acquire combined basic state pensions and state second pensions that bring their incomes over the pension credit threshold. What is now proposed are two changes, one that the scheme will evolve into one offering a flat-rate pension, the other that the opt-out option will be eliminated. What therefore this means is that the White Paper holds out the prospect of evolution by about 2030 to a situation in which the combination of what will then be two flat-rate contributory state pensions amounts to an income above the pension credit level for a significant number of people, thereby achieving its objective of reducing dependence on the latter.

So in the face of two demands from radical critics of the UK pension system for:

- the uprating of the basic pension to above the pension credit level;
- the elimination of complex social insurance qualifying rules;

what is offered is:

- a very long-term programme to, in effect, bring up the basic pension by combining it with the State Second Pension;
- some lightening of social insurance rules but no shift away from contributions, rather a subtle measure to increase contributions for some.

The elimination of the opt-out will put every employee on the same footing, generating a situation in which it will be mainly social insurance rather than tax that will pay for the increase in the state pension for all. Broadly this may be seen as a progressive measure: all will pay through income-related contributions for an enhanced flat-rate benefit. However, since the alternative would have been pension improvement through the ordinary tax system it needs to be pointed out that the current Chancellor of the Exchequer's obsession with avoiding obvious direct tax increases is contributing once again to a situation in which, in the UK, 'National Insurance' is simply tax by another name. It is a tax moreover that is, in itself, not particularly progressive as it is subject to a cap well before the top end of the income distribution. Significantly, moreover, it must be noted that reducing the qualifying period for some does not reduce the period over which National Insurance contributions must be paid. They go on until the official pension age for all in employment, and will thus need to be paid for longer by women when the already coming pension age change occurs and by all once the age change proposed in the White Paper occurs (see below).

In this context the administrative implications of all this are by no means trivial. The elaborate system of tax records over a working life, accompanied by complex crediting rules, is being maintained more or less solely for the operation of the pension system. The White Paper in fact explicitly rejected the alternative of a citizens pension, where every citizen would have a right to an appropriate flat-rate pension after a specific age, with the argument that a 'big bang' shift to it would be too costly and a gradual shift to it too complex.

One final aspect of the reform proposal must not be left unmentioned. The plan is that there should be upward shifts of the pension age, by changes of one year in each of 2024, 2034 and 2044. These, of course, imply public expenditure savings (fewer pensions and more contributions). Elsewhere in the White Paper there are general observations on what the government is doing and might do to encourage longer working lives on a voluntary basis. The Trades Union Congress (TUC, 2006, p 10, para 4.4) attacked this proposal, arguing:

> that differences in life expectancy mean that an across-the-board increase in the pension age would affect the poor the most. Further, an increase in state pension age would have little impact on the retirement age of the better off, so it would be those on lower incomes who would be more likely to work longer to pay for better pensions.

While there clearly is a case for accepting in principle the case for longer working lives today, the TUC's argument raises two issues.

One is whether or not there might be a case for an approach to pension age that took into account the length of a working life, bearing in mind that the better off tend to join the workforce later, rather than using a specific retirement age. The problem about this, however, is that it lays undue emphasis upon time in employment as the basis for the determination of pension entitlement, something that has been questioned at various places in this book. The other is the issue about the contrast between actual retirement ages and pension qualifying ages, discussed in Chapter Five. The TUC case seems to accept that the consequence of a change in the pension age will be more years in employment, something questioned in Chapter Six. Finally, it should be noted that while the journalistic response to this change is to stress that people will have to work longer for the state pension, the reality is complex since, as noted, such a statement disregards the issue of when we start our workforce participation and also the government is in fact relaxing the rules related to the numbers of years in employment for full state pension entitlement.

These proposals are, at the time of writing, the subject of legislation; the implementation timetable envisaged will extend over a rather long period. When exactly the legislation on personal savings accounts is to be introduced is not stated but the government does say (DWP, 2006, p 16) that it will be introduced in 2012. There is a great deal of detailed work still to be done on this. A similar timetable is proposed for the rest of the agenda, including the quite simple change in the uprating principle.

Since by the time this book is published the government will probably be steering its legislation through Parliament without significant changes, it might be assumed that the UK pensions debate is now closed. This is by no means the case. The day the proposal to legislate was mentioned in the Queen's Speech one critic was quoted as saying 'This is a clever exercise in trying to persuade people that something generous is being done when the truth is it isn't. The government is rearranging the deckchairs but not making state pensions more generous' (*The Guardian*, 16 November 2006, quoting Ros Altmann). The debate will go on.

In fact there is scope for change even within the implementation of the legislation. It provides very much a bare framework for change, with much detail still to be filled in. In the case of the change to the uprating principle it should be noted that pension rates are changed every year and the present legislation does not prevent a more generous increase in the rates; the current linking to prices only determines the minimum. Hence, it is quite possible to bring the change forward, or to uprate even more generously than in terms of the wage rate change in any one year so as to increase the upward movement towards the equivalent of the 1979 level. The objection to this is, of course, the cost, which it would be impractical to brush aside as a consideration. On the other hand, the provision of a government contribution to the pension savings scheme will entail costs. This has been noted above as an equivalent of the tax relief provided to existing private pensions. One way in which more resources could be found to support the state pension would be by cutting this. Sinfield (2007) draws attention to the size of this sum, now over £14 billion. It is very considerable and regressive in impact, as more goes to those making higher contributions, with very much of it offsetting the higher (40%) rate of tax.

Conclusions

As was stated at the very beginning of this book it is not going to finish with a presentation of an ideal pension scheme. The concern throughout it has been, while offering a critical perspective and a readiness to challenge conventional assumptions about pensions and particularly about predictions of a future crisis, to accept that pension systems are created in a political world in which interests clash, past decisions create 'pathways' for future ones and the politics of pensions has the peculiar characteristic of being concerned with future needs and problems as well as current ones in a political system where present orientation dominates decision making. Any changes to already elaborate pension systems in which many individuals have already made contributions and formed expectations are likely to be incremental and will probably be small. Only perhaps in those societies designing public pension systems for the first time will there be any possibility of choices between a broad range of options, and even in those societies there will be some existing interests (notably – as was pointed out in Chapter One – the fact that the state has already some commitments to its own employees).

Nevertheless, throughout the book it has been emphasised that there are some important issues at stake. These are particularly about the extent to which there is a dominant perspective on pensions that sees them as payments to be earned through regular labour market participation. This point has been stressed as an issue for women: 'Pensioners are women and pensions are for women, pension policy has been designed for men' (Hollis, 2005, col 502). True enough but this can be further generalised to the proposition that pension policy has been designed for labour market participants. Those women who get the most from the system are those who have been able to participate fully, all or most of their lives, in the labour force. Turning that the other way round, and putting it in gender-neutral terms, it can be said that those who make the most of their contributions to society in other ways – particularly in caring roles – get the least from the system. It should be noted here that I have been at pains in various places to use 'employees' or the more awkward expression 'labour market participants' because so often 'workers' is used in this context as if there is no other work.

Those considerations extend beyond the issues about how pension entitlements are determined. It is hoped that Chapter Six of this book is seen not just as an attack on simplistic generalisations from demography but also as a challenge to a view of society in which people are designated as 'dependent' if they are not labour market participants, and pensioners are particularly seen as a group who make no contribution to society. Issues about work–life balance are on the modern political agenda (well, just about on the margins of the agenda), issues about how people contribute to pensions is part of that agenda, so too should be issues about when retirement occurs and how people are enabled to continue 'living'.

As far, then, as specific issues about pensions are concerned, it seems useful to structure considerations of the issues about pensions in terms of the concepts of tiers used by the OECD. The issues about the first tier go directly to questions about ensuring that everyone has an adequate income in old age. It is important to do that in ways that do not operate to deter self-provision. It must be acknowledged that there is a problem about perspectives that seem to involve imposing levels of equality after pension age that have not existed before that age. That does not mean that the reduction of inequalities in society is an undesirable goal – indeed, levels of inequality are much too high and have been allowed to increase excessively – only that this issue must be addressed across the board, not seen as a core issue for pension policy. Our expectations of incomes in old age are generated by our expectations earlier in life. In any case it would not be practical politics to attack those expectations.

Two points that may potentially seem to conflict follow from that last proposition. One is that if an adequate first-tier pension is to be provided, some measure of progressivity (as noted earlier, what is meant here – contrary to the emphasis in the last paragraph – is some redistribution that narrows the spread of incomes at least from the bottom end) is inevitable. The other is that it is important that a state-guaranteed minimum pension is not provided in ways that deter, or are seen to be unjust by, those who make arrangements for themselves. To avoid any conflict between these two principles a good first-tier pension needs to be funded by taxation (that is by *all*, not generated from redistribution within a contributory pension system). It also needs to be available to all, that is a floor position from which all other pensions provisions start. What is embodied in this proposition is the need both for the absence of direct means-tests governing entitlement to a basic pension, and the avoidance of more subtle devices that (as, for example, in the Swedish system described in Chapter Three) have a not dissimilar effect inasmuch as other pension entitlements are wholly or partly offset against the basic provision.

What is being set out here is the case for the basic or 'citizens pension' approach to a first-tier pension. The UK White Paper (DWP, 2006) sets out arguments against this in terms of problems about a transition to it that are a combination of administrative expediency and potential unfairness. The UK government is obviously motivated by concerns about the cost (transitional unfairness depends very much upon the ultimate levels of benefit chosen) and by the implications for other taxation of a transparent shift away from National Insurance funding (a topic already explored in the discussion of its plans above).

The case for 'basic' or 'citizens' incomes, tax-funded rather than insurance funded, and guaranteed to all, has been made in a variety of texts. The conventional argument against such benefits is that they may deter labour market participation. The strength of that argument depends upon the level of benefits involved. However, in the case of pensions, if the qualifying age is set at a level where either it is generally accepted that labour market participation is not expected or it is not feasible for most people, that argument has no validity. On the contrary, it may make some forms of labour market participation easier than with current arrangements, particularly where means-tests deter this.

The issue of the level of benefit is obviously important. It would not be appropriate to suggest a level here. Any figure given would date during the life of the book. In the UK some of the trouble with the existing system stems from past decisions that set the standard social insurance pension level too low. The pension credit represents in this respect an advance. However, there is still a need to consider higher levels inasmuch as there is likely to continue to be a substantial group of people unable to establish any other pension entitlement. While conventionally this is an issue about the feasibility of pushing female labour market participation up to much higher levels, it is preferable to express this in terms of the concern expressed above that people who make valuable contributions to society other than through labour market participation (with unpaid care for others as far and away the most salient example) should not be neglected in old age.

The last word needed on the first tier of the pension system concerns the issue about 'who qualifies'. The term 'citizens pension' has been used here alongside the concept of a basic pension. This usage is simply an adoption of prevailing terminology (for example the White Paper uses it). Such a usage poses certain problems in relation to what is meant by citizenship. That could be manipulated in ways that would exclude substantial numbers of people. It is not appropriate to go deeply into the subject of citizenship here; it is a topic that it is hoped another book in this series will address. It has been noted in Chapter Three that New Zealand uses 'residence' for a specific period to define entitlement. Any approach to qualification rules in the UK would need to take into account the relatively free movement of people within the European Union and the fact that the UK receives substantial numbers of migrants at various stages in their lives (note how some discussions of demographic change see this as important for the UK's economy). There have been some efforts to secure benefit entitlement portability across the European Union. It looks at the present time as if substantial equalisation of social security across the European Union is a utopian dream. Certainly the UK system stands as one of the crucial barriers to that development since contributory social insurance is such a weak element in its system. That makes the issue of protection of recent residents all the more important.

Turning now to the issues about the second tier, the starting point for a discussion of this has to be the debate between state PAYG schemes on the one hand and private funded ones on the other. The arguments against the funding approach were explored in Chapter Seven, examining the 'universalist' case made by Korpi and Palme (1998) and Myles' (2002) exploration of ways to achieve a fair deal between the generations.

It would be wrong, however, simply to argue the case for social insurance using the PAYG approach as if it solved all the problems of reaching a goal of adequate pensions for all. The very reason for having a first tier in pension systems flows from difficulties in achieving this. Modifications to social insurance, writing in contributions from those unable to participate fully in the labour force, now feature in all the most inclusive schemes, yet it is still the case that more could be done to compensate for disadvantages flowing from limited access to employment, or part-time employment or poorly paid employment.

It was noted in Chapter Seven that the approach to social insurance adopted in the UK never took a rigorous form, unlike the German pension scheme. While therefore – in the context of the politics of the European Union – it is to be hoped that the UK will not participate in any challenge to the use of that model, it is not practical to suggest that such a comprehensive form of second tier pension system should be established here too. The last opportunity to do that disappeared with the adoption of a limited supplementary pension scheme for those without private pensions in the 1970s.

So that, then, brings the policy debate for the UK back to either strengthening basic pensions and letting the tax-subsidised private pension sector run on as the voluntary alternative or seeking (like the proposals in the White Paper) to arrive at ways of securing wider public participation in the private sector.

The White Paper proposals have much to commend them in this respect, with their emphasis on employer and government subsidy, government regulation and efforts to minimise administrative costs. The government has rejected compulsion but suggested a peculiar form of inertia selling, putting all employees in the scheme unless they opt out. That hardly seems to fit with an increasing emphasis in relation to many public services of being quite explicit about the contract between the provider and the recipient. There is a danger that some employers will seek to deter their employees from joining a scheme that imposes costs on them too. There does seem to be a case for compulsion, but only if accompanied by other conditions listed below:

- There is a need for government guarantees in respect of pensions to be quite explicit, with the promise of subsidy if private schemes cannot fulfil those.

- There should be attention to introducing into this tier of the pension system some of the devices, mentioned above in the context of social insurance schemes, to enable people outside the labour force to secure credits. These would have to be provided by the government. The White Paper makes much of a more generous approach to the basic state pension in this respect but disregards this issue for the new pension savings scheme.

- If there are to be choices between funds for investors, and a default fund of some kind as in Sweden, why cannot there be a public investment fund as an option. In Chapter Seven Blackburn's (2002) views on this were reported, suggesting a new approach to state control over enterprise. What is proposed here is less ambitious. Why cannot we have the option – guaranteed in the terms specified in the first of my points here – to invest in our hospitals, schools and so on? After all, much private investment is made more secure through partial investment in government funds.

The discussion of the UK White Paper, in the last section, ended with some scepticism about what would actually happen. There seems a distinct danger that little will happen, or that the new savings scheme will come in as another limited incremental measure – like stakeholder pensions – that will make little or no difference to the distribution of resources in later life described in Chapter Four. If that is the case then a key focus for lobbyists concerned to improve pensions should be a move to a much better first-tier system in the UK. It has been interesting to note how the case for this has increasingly come to be made not only by the organisations dispassionately concerned about the welfare of pensioners but also by private sector organisations who have recognised that the pension credit system makes it more difficult to sell private investments to people with modest incomes.

It would be good to be able to argue for an approach to pension reform that would stop the issue being a 'political football'. Frankly, observing a rather similar debate that surfaces from time to time about trying to do this for the National Health Service, there are grounds for doubt about whether this is feasible. Again, even compared to the US, let alone Germany, the UK has gone down a pathway which makes it very difficult to achieve this. The 1940s' reforms seemed to suggest that a sort of PAYG-based fund (it is assumed that at this stage in the book readers will understand that this does not mean full funding, but rather arrangements like those that were supposed to be used in the US to protect surpluses) was being set up. A variety of political decisions – initially a commitment to paying out pensions too soon, later a variety of shifts in respect of the relationship between contributions and benefits and then the abandonment of a notional government contribution to the fund – together with the Treasury's propensity to blur the distinctions between different income streams and their purposes, destroyed this. An alternative pathway might have been set up had the system been given independent management arrangements, with outside participation from employees and employers. It was not; hence we have a system easily manipulated by central government.

Hence, stability in respect of the first tier of the system may be very difficult to achieve. It is, then, important to look at ways of building better protection of existing systems into second-tier arrangements. As far as existing parts of this tier are concerned, the shifts of schemes from defined benefit bases to defined contribution bases require attention. As suggested earlier, one of the issues about fairness that is important is about expectations. People who enter into work contracts to which pension arrangements are attached have a right to expect that the latter will be honoured. It has been particularly disturbing to see governments wriggling to try to get out of 'implied' contracts with their own employees by trying to change pension rules and modify defined benefit arrangements. The private sector has complained that when government backed off such change, it was looking after its own. But really the issues are about the government honouring commitments to its employees.

I want to end, notwithstanding my reluctance to take too utopian a stance, on the underlying theme of Chapter Six. This is that the whole pensions debate is dominated by an economic perspective that not only treats both needs and contributions to society as secondary considerations, but which even in its own terms uses micro- rather than macro-economic assumptions that individualise issues. Hence, it pays little attention to the impact of demand on labour market participation and contributes to perspectives that mistakenly assume that societies can somehow store money away to protect themselves against demographic change.

References

Arber, S. and Ginn, J. (2004) 'Ageing and gender: diversity and change', *Social Trends*, no 34, pp 11-14.

Barr, N. (2001) *The Welfare State as Piggy Bank*, Oxford: Oxford University Press.

Barr, N. (2002) 'The Pension Puzzle', *Economic Issues*, no 29, New York: International Monetary Fund.

Beattie, R. and McGillivray, W. (1995) 'A risky strategy: reflections on the World Bank report, *Averting the Old Age Crisis*', *International Social Security Review*, vol 48, no 3/4, pp 5-22.

Beveridge, W. (1942) *Social Insurance and Allied Services*, Cmd 6404, London: HMSO.

Blackburn, R. (2002) *Banking on Death*, London: Verso.

Bonoli, G. and Shinkawa, T. (eds) (2005) *Ageing and Pension Reform Around the World*, Cheltenham: Elgar.

Casey, B., Oxley, H., Whitehouse, E., Antolin, P., Duval, R. and Leibfritz, W. (2003) *Policies for an Ageing Society: Recent Measures and Areas for Further Reform*, Economics Department Working Paper 369, Paris: OECD.

DWP (Department for Work and Pensions) (2006) *Security in Retirement: Towards a New Pensions System*, White Paper, Cm 6841, London: DWP.

European Commission (2003) *The Social Situation in the European Union 2003*, Luxembourg: European Commission.

European Commission (2004) *The Social Situation in the European Union 2004*, Luxembourg: European Commission.

Field, F. (2006) 'Why has it all gone wrong? The past, present and future of British pensions', in H. Pemberton, P. Thane and N. Whiteside (eds) *Britain's Pension Crisis: History and Policy*, Oxford: Oxford University Press, pp 140-4.

Fredericks, P., Maier, R. and de Graaf, W. (2006) 'Shifting the pension mix: consequences for Dutch and Danish women', *Social Policy and Administration*, vol 40, no 5, pp 475-92.

Fritzell, J. and Lennartson, C. (2005) 'Financial transfers between generations in Sweden', *Ageing and Society*, vol 25, no 3, pp 397-414.

Gee, E.M. and Gutman, G.M. (eds) (2000) *The Overselling of Population Ageing*, Don Mills, Ontario: Oxford University Press.

Guardian, The (2006) 'Pensioners groups call for urgent action on reforms', http://business.guardian.co.uk/story/0,,1948916,00.html#article_continue

Hantrais, L. (2004) *Family Policy Matters*, Bristol: The Policy Press.

Hollis, P. (Baroness) (2005) *Hansard*, HL Deb, 25 May, col 502.

James, E. (2001) 'Comments on rethinking pension reform: 10 myths about social security systems', in R. Holzmann and J. Siglitz (eds) *New Ideas about Social Security: Towards Sustainable Pensions Systems in the Twenty-first Century*, Washington, DC: World Bank, pp 63-70.

Kedward, R. (2006) *La Vie en Bleu: France and the French since 1900*, London: Penguin Books.

Kingdon, J.W. (1995) *Agendas, Alternatives and Public Policies* (2nd edition; 1st edition 1984), New York: Addison, Wesley, Longman.

Kohli, M., Rein, M., Guillemard, A.-M. and Van Gunsteren, H. (1991) *Time for Retirement: Comparative Studies of Early Exit from the Labour Force*, Cambridge: Cambridge University Press.

Korpi, W. and Palme, J. (1998) 'The paradox of redistribution: welfare state institutions and poverty in the western countries', *American Sociological Review*, vol 63, no 5, pp 661-87.

Lynes, T. (1997) 'The British case', in M. Rein and E. Wadensjö (eds) *Enterprise and the Welfare State*, Cheltenham: Edward Elgar, pp 309-51.

Macnicol, J. (2006) *Age Discrimination: An Historical and Contemporary Analysis*, Cambridge: Cambridge University Press.

Meurer, A. (2001) 'Current developments in German old-age provision: reconciling continuity and change', *International Social Security Review*, vol 54, pp 111-17.

Middleton, R. (2000) *The British Economy since 1945: Engaging with the Debate*, Basingstoke: Palgrave.

Mullan, P. (2005) *Ageing and the 'Pensions Crisis'*, 8 December, www.spiked-online.com

Myles, J. (2002) 'A new social contract for the elderly?', in G. Esping-Andersen (ed) *Why We Need a New Welfare State*, Oxford: Oxford University Press.

National Statistics (2005) *Pensioners Income Series 2003-4*, London: The Stationery Office.

OECD (Organisation for Economic Co-operation and Development) (2005a) *Pensions at a Glance: Public Policies across OECD Countries*, Paris: OECD.

OECD (2005b) *Pension Markets in Focus*, Paris: OECD.

OECD (2005c) *Social Expenditure Database*, Paris: OECD.

Pensions Commission (2004) *Pensions: Challenges and Choices. The First Report of the Pensions Commission*, London: The Stationery Office.

Pensions Commission (2005) *A New Pensions Settlement for the Twenty-first Century. The Second Report of the Pensions Commission*, London: The Stationery Office.

Sainsbury, D. (1996) *Gender Equality and Welfare States*, Cambridge: Cambridge University Press.

Sinfield, A. (2007) 'Occupational welfare', in M. Powell (ed) *Understanding the Mixed Economy of Welfare*, Bristol: The Policy Press, pp 129-48.

Stiglitz, J. (2005) 'No free lunches for pensioners', *The Guardian*, 19 April.

Thane, P. (2000) *Old Age in English History*, Oxford: Oxford University Press.

TUC (Trades Union Congress) (2006) *TUC Responses to the Pensions White Paper*.

United Nations (2003) *World Population Prospects*, New York: United Nations.

Whiteford, P. and Whitehouse, E. (2006) 'Pension challenges and pension reforms in OECD countries', *Oxford Review of Economic Policy*, vol 22, no 1, pp 78-94.

Whiteside, N. (2006) 'Occupational pensions and the search for security', in H. Pemberton, P. Thane and N. Whiteside (eds) *Britain's Pension Crisis: History and Policy*, Oxford: Oxford University Press, pp 125-39.

World Bank (1994) *Averting the Old Age Crisis*, Oxford: Oxford University Press.

A

adequacy of pensions, 16, 17, 30, 34, 37, Chapter 3, 71, 88, 94, 100, 131, 132, 133, 153, 154, 155, 159, 162, 168, 170
ageing populations, 6, 118-122, 123
annuities, 36, 43, 78, 95
assets, 4, 24, 34, 37, 54, 61, 74, 78, 79, 83, 84, 89, 90, 99, 130, 131-2, 140, 141, 148, 151
Australia, 11, 13, 47, 48, 85, 87, 89, 90, 97-8, 101, 108, 120, 122, 124, 156
Austria, 53, 62, 85, 108, 109, 119, 120, 122, 124, 125, 136, 156

B

Belgium, 53, 62, 85, 108, 119, 120, 122, 124, 125, 136, 156
Beveridge Report, 25-8, 29, 30, 32, 33, 39, 64, 65, 67, 68, 74, 151, 171
burden of caring, 60

C

Canada, 108, 109, 113, 120, 122, 124, 156
carers; caring tasks, 31, 60, 65, 73, 112, 123, 132
charitable organisations; charities, 4, 8, 23, 24
child care, 60, 65
Chile, 15, 101, 102
China, 15, 128, 148
citizens pensions, 72, 97, 164, 169-70
crediting in contributions, 65, 94, 162, 164, 168-90
cutting public pension commitments, 12-13, 14, 66, 97, 154, 157
Czech Republic, 120, 122, 124

D

defined benefit systems, 36, 38, 44, 58, 63, 71, 75, 76, 77, 79, 81, 82, 85, 86, 87, 91, 95, 97, 100, 101, 173
defined contribution systems, 37, 44, 58, 67, 71, 75, 76, 78, 82, 85, 86, 95, 101, 147, 155, 173
demand for labour, 127, 128, 134
demographic changes, 7, 18, 20, 88, 95, 104, 110, 116, Chapter 6, 135, 136, 137, 138, 140, 147, 148, 149, 152, 154, 155, 159, 170, 174
'demographic time bomb', 20, 104, 116, Chapter 6, 135
Denmark, 13, 53, 62, 85, 87, 90, 102, 108, 120, 122, 124, 125, 136, 156
disabled people, 55, 73, 108, 114, 162
disincentive effects; disincentives to pension saving, 26, 35, 37, 65, 159-60
divorce, 63, 64

E

early retirement, 18, 110, 111-14
Eastern Europe, 15
economic growth, 36, 79, 129, 142, 145
emigration, 119
Europe, 7, 52, 53, 61, 62, 63, 64, 119, 121, 125, 136, 138, 144, 151, 152, 155, 156, 170, 171

F

falling birth rate, 118, 148
final salary-based pension schemes, 28, 36, 37, *see also* 'defined benefit systems'

Finland, 53, 62, 108, 113, 119, 120, 122, 124, 125, 136, 156
flat-rate pensions, 25, 26, 28, 30, 31, 33, 44, 46, 72, 85, 91, 100, 101, 156, 158, 163, 164
France, 11, 13, 47, 53, 62, 83, 85, 86, 87, 89, 90, 108, 109, 113, 114, 120, 122, 124, 125, 136, 144, 156
fuel costs, 53, 54, 56
funding, 18, 20, 31, 32, 37, 71, 72, 76, 77, 78-82, 84, 86, 92, 94, 95-7, 98, 99, 101, 131, 134, Chapter 7, 154, 157-8, 168, 169, 170, 173

G

Germany, 10, 11, 13, 47, 48, 53, 62, 83, 85, 86, 89, 90, 91, 92-4, 95, 101, 108, 113, 120, 122, 124, 125, 136, 138, 143, 144, 145, 150, 151, 154, 156, 158, 171, 173
graduated pensions, 29, 30, 38, 44, 100, 101, 162
Greece, 53, 62, 108, 120, 124, 125, 136, 155, 156
Gross Domestic Product (GDP), 132, 136, 137, 156
guarantee credit, *see* 'pension credit' *and* 'minimum income guarantee'

H

health and care costs, 53
housing costs, 51, 52, 54
Hungary, 108, 120, 122, 124

I

ill health, 24, 73, 112, 114, 123
immigration, 119, 127
individual accounts, 92, 139, 144, *see also* 'notional accounts'
inflation, 11, 30, 35, 36, 44, 78, 140, 148

insurance, 8, 9, 10, 11, 12, 14, 15, 24, 25, 26, 27, 28, 30, 31, 32, 35, 39, 64, 65, 71, 73, 74, 75, 77, 78, 89, 92, 93, 94, 96, 101, 138, 143, 144, 150, 152, 154, 163, 169, 170, 172
investment, 8, 9, 15, 16, 30, 33, 36, 37, 38, 43, 77, 78, 79, 80, 82, 83, 84, 86, 87, 91, 99, 101, 135, 139, 140, 141, 143, 144, 145, 146, 147, 148, 149, 151, 158, 161, 172
Ireland, 53, 62, 108, 120, 122, 124, 125
Italy, 53, 62, 85, 87, 89, 90, 108, 113, 120, 122, 124, 125, 136, 156

J

Japan, 47, 85, 90, 108, 113, 119, 120, 122, 124, 145, 156

K

Korea, South, 85, 119, 120, 122, 128

L

labour market, 9, 11, 16, 30, 36, 43, 63, 64, 65, 73, 108, 109, 112, 114, 123, 125, 126, 127, 130, 133, 167, 169
labour market participation, 11, 16, 30, 60, 63, 64, 112, 114, 123, 125-7, 169, 171
life expectancy, 7, 14, 61, 66, 67, 121, 126, 148
low-paid workers, 13, 31, 36, 45, 49, 57
Luxembourg, 136

M

male breadwinner model, 64-5
marriage, 60, 64-8, 96, 121

means-testing; means-tests, 4, 11, 15, 24, 25, 33, 35, 37, 50, 53, 54, 55, 56, 59, 60, 64-8, 72, 74, 75, 91, 94, 95, 96, 97, 98, 133, 148, 156, 158, 160, 161

Mexico, 124

minimum income guarantee, 33, 34, 35, 36, 37, 85, 98, *see also* 'pension credit'

minimum pension age, *see* 'pension age'

N

National Insurance, 26, 27, 31, 34, 35, 38, 60, 83, 85, 163, 164, 169

Netherlands, 47, 48, 53, 62, 65, 67, 85, 87, 89, 90, 96-7, 100, 101, 113, 120, 122, 124, 125, 136, 156

New Zealand, 47, 48, 85, 86, 90, 98, 100, 108, 120, 122, 124, 156, 170

Norway, 13, 84, 108, 113, 120, 122, 124

notional accounts, 75, 85, 95, see also 'individual accounts'

O

occupational pensions, 28, 29, 32, 38, 50, 96

Organisation for Economic Co-operation and Development (OECD), 45, 47, 71, 72, 74, 75, 76, 84, 85, 86, 90, 95, 97, 100, 102, 113, 120, 123, 124, 136, 138, 154, 155, 156, 168

owner-occupied housing, 54, 74, 148, 149

P

part-time work, 32, 61, 62, 63, 65, 105, 125, 126, 161, 171

'pay-as-you-go' (PAYG) pensions, 30, 71, 76, 77, 82, 83, 84, 91, 93, 94, 97, 131, 141, 142, 145, 149, 150, 152, 157, 158, 170, 173

pension age, 2, 44, 81, 103, 104, 107, 108, 109, 110, 111, 115, 118, 125, 127, 160, 164, 165, 168

pension contributions, 2, 4, 9, 12, 14, 15, 25, 27, 28, 29-30, 31, 35, 37, 38, 39, 42, 43, 48, 58, 59, 60, 61, 65, 68, 73, 75, 77, 78-84, 88, 89, 91, 92, 93, 94, 95, 96, 97, 101, 104, 109, 130, 131, 132, Chapter 7, 157, 159, 161-2, 163, 164, 166, 167, 169, 170, 173, 174

pension credit, 33-5, 37, 38, 45, 51, 52, 54, 58, 59, 60, 66, 91, 97, 98, 158, 159, 160, 162, 163, 169, *see also* 'minimum income guarantee

pension funds, *see* 'funding'

pensions legislation in the UK 2006-07, 39, 159-66

pension 'pillars', 37, 76, 76, 77, 95, 96, 102, 158, *see also* 'pension tiers'

pension portability, 63, 79, 119

pension 'tiers', 37, 38, 49, 67, 71-7, 84, 85, 86, 87, 91, 95, 96, 97, 98, 100, 101, 143, 168, 169, 170, 172, 173

pension uprating, 27, 31, 33, 34, 162, 165, 166

pensions arrangements for women, 7, 17, 27, 28, 30, 31, 32, 33, 36, 38, 43, 45, 46, 51, 56, 57, 60-8, 73, 94, 105, 106, 109, 111, 112, 114, 123, 125, 126, 129, 130, 132, 162, 164, 167, 169

Poland, 108, 109, 119, 120, 122, 124

policy pathways, 1, 2, 12, 17, 26, 39, 151, 153, 166, 171, 173

Poor Law, the, 8, 9, 23, 24

Portugal, 53, 62, 108, 124, 125, 136

poverty, 6, 8, 10, 11, 12, 13, 16, 24, 29, 34, 39, 41, 42, 48, 49, 50, 51, 52, 53-6, 60, 68, 77, 81, 88, 156, 159, 160, 164

private pensions, 2, 6, 9, 12, 13, 14, 16, 19, 24, 25, 26, 28, 29, 30, 31, 32-3, 34, 35-7, 38, 39, 49, 50, 51, 52, 57, 58, 59, 61, 63, 64, 66, 67, 68, 69, 77-84, 86, 89, 92, 94, 98, 99, 101, 106, 108, 110, 111, 112, 115, 131, 135, 137, 138, 141, 145-6, 149, 150, 153, 159, 160-1, 162, 166, 171

provident funds, 15, 77, 98, 100

public employees, 5, 20, 23, 25, 31, 32, 36, 51, 57, 79, 134, 138, 157

R

replacement rates, 41, 42, 44, 45, 46, 47, 48, 74, 94, 98

retirement, 3, 4, 7, 17, 18, 23, 24, 25, 26, 34, 36, 43, 44, 49, 58, 60, 87, 95, 97, 99, Chapter 5, 119, 126, 127, 129, 131, 143, 151, 159, 164, 165, 167

S

Scandinavia, 11, 66, 133

self-employment, 59, 105

self-help, 8, 9, 23, 24

sickness, *see* 'ill health'

Singapore, 15, 77, 98-100, 101

Slovak Republic, 120, 124

social assistance, 24, 25, 26, 28, 34, 35, 72, 74, 95, 98, *see also* 'means-testing'

social care, 55, 57, 131, 132, 133, 148

social insurance, 10, 11, 14, 15, 24, 25-8, 29, 31, 39, 64, 65, 74-5, 77, 89, 92-4, 101, 138, 143, 144, 150, 154, 163, 169, 170, 172, *see also* 'National Insurance'

Social Security Act 1973, 29

Social Security Pensions Act of 1975, 29

Spain, 53, 62, 85, 108, 113, 120, 122, 124, 125, 136, 155, 156

stakeholder pensions, 33, 35, 36, 37, 38, 160, 172

State Earnings Related Pension Scheme (SERPS) (UK), 30, 31, 32, 33, 38, 162

State Second Pension (UK), 33, 35, 38, 45, 54, 59, 66, 87, 158, 162, 163

stock markets, 37, 10, 146

subsistence level, 26, 162

Sweden, 13, 47, 48, 53, 62, 65, 75, 77, 84, 85, 87, 90, 95-6, 101, 102, 108, 113, 120, 122, 124, 125, 126, 131, 135, 136, 143, 144, 146, 154, 156, 158, 161, 168, 172

Switzerland, 108, 120, 122, 124, 156

T

Taiwan, 108

tax, 20, 31, 33, 37, 38, 42, 43, 60, 72, 73, 74, 78, 81, 83, 92, 94, 98, 108, 109, 131, 138, 141, 142, 143, 147, 151, 154, 161, 163, 164, 166, 168, 169, 171

tax concessions, 33, 94, 98, 108

trades unions, 12

TUC, 164, 165

Turkey, 108

U

UK Pensions Commission 2004-05, 19, 20, 28, 34, 38, 39, 54, 56, 57, 58, 59, 66, 81, 82, 84, 95, 96, 97, 98, 100, 114, 115, 121, 126, 127, 129, 130, 131, 136, 138, 141, 142, 144, 148, 158, 159, 160

UK Pensions White Paper 2006, 19, 39, 158, 159, 160, 161, 162, 163, 164, 169, 170, 171, 172

unemployment, 24, 30, 49, 73, 92, 95, 112, 114, 147
universalism in social policy, 13, 150, 170
unremunerated roles, 132
US, 7, 10, 11, 28, 47, 48, 65, 82, 84, 85, 89, 90, 91-2, 98, 101, 102, 108, 113, 120, 122, 124, 146, 156, 173

W

wealth, *see* 'assets'
widows, 28, 61
working-age population, 57, 123, 124
work–life balance, 17, 18, 167
World Bank, 10, 39, 76, 77, 87, 96, 101, 135, 144, 145, 146